THE CHINESE BLACK CHAMBER

Other books by Herbert O. Yardley

The American Black Chamber

Yardleygrams

The Blonde Countess

Red Sun of Nippon

Crows Are Black Everywhere
(with Carl Grabo)

The Education of a Poker Player

THE CHINESE BLACK CHAMBER

An Adventure in Espionage

Herbert O. Yardley

Houghton Mifflin Company
Boston 1983

7/10/87

4

Library of Congress Cataloging in Publication Data

Yardley, Herbert O. (Herbert Osborn), 1889–1958.
  The Chinese black chamber

Chinese title on added t.p.: Chung-kuo hei shih.
  1. Sino-Japanese Conflict, 1937–1945 — Secret service
— China. 2. Sino-Japanese Conflict, 1937–1945 —
Personal narratives, American. 3. Yardley, Herbert O.
(Herbert Osborn), 1889–1958. I. Title. II. Title:
Chung-kuo hei shih.
DS777.533.S65Y37 1983   940.53   83-8562
ISBN 0-395-34648-7

Printed in the United States of America

Q 10 9 8 7 6 5 4 3 2 1

CONTENTS

- Introduction
  by James Bamford   vii

- Cast of Characters   xxv

- The Chinese
  Black Chamber   3

- Memories of The American
  Black Chamber
  by Edna Ramsaier
  Yardley   221

INTRODUCTION
by James Bamford

Twenty miles north of Washington, D.C., on more than a thousand acres of Fort George G. Meade, the largest intelligence organization in the free world makes its home. Created in total secrecy by President Truman in 1952, the National Security Agency quietly diverts many of the world's private, commercial, diplomatic, and military communications into a hidden city of nearly two dozen heavily guarded buildings of brick, glass, and cement. One, the Headquarters-Operations complex, is soon to become the second biggest single building in the entire federal government. Only the Pentagon is larger.

Buried deep in the bowels of the Headquarters-Operations Building is the largest concentration of computers on earth; the space taken up by the supermachines is measured not by the square foot, but by the acre. Here, on thin, laser-recorded optical discs, each containing more than a hundred billion bits of information, and on thousands of miles of magnetic tape, is the counterpart of Jorge Luis Borges's fabled infinite library, in which all of the planet's knowledge and information reside, maddeningly encoded.

To unscramble these complex ciphers the NSA relies on such computers as the CRAY-1, which has a memory unit capable of transferring up to 320 million words per second, or the equivalent of about twenty-five-hundred 300-page books; and on laser printers, which can place those words on endless miles of paper at the rate of 22,000 lines per minute. And soon to be put into practical form by NSA's Research and Engineering Organization are such strange-sounding concepts as Josephson Junction technology, magnetic bubbles, analog optical computing technology, and light-sound interaction and charge-transfer devices, which will be capable of performing more than one quadrillion (or 1,000,000,000,000,000) operations a second.

But long before there was a CRAY-1 or even an NSA, there was simply a young man with nothing more than a sharp mind and very farsighted vision. His name was Herbert Osborn Yardley.

In the black and gray world of espionage and codebreaking, Herbert O. Yardley was a Calder mobile of bright bold colors. He was a free spirit in a land of cenobites. Born on April 13, 1889, in the small southwestern Indiana town of Worthington, young Yardley would later develop a talent for unscrambling foreign codes and ciphers that may well have grown from a far less clandestine but equally challenging (and possibly more profitable) avocation: poker. When he was not running for president of his high school class, editing the school paper, and acting as captain of the football team, he could usually be found in a saloon called Monty's Place, picking up pointers from Old Salty East and Mont Mull, or else at one of the other ten saloons or three poolrooms in Worthington.

Following high school, Yardley went off to the University of Chicago, but left after only a year and returned to Worthington to work as a railroad telegrapher. He had learned the trade from his father, who was employed as a railroad agent. But soon the monotony of tapping out freight delays and passenger reservations began to dull his spirit, and in 1912, at the age of twenty-three, he passed his telegraph key to someone else and climbed aboard a train bound for Washington's Union Station.

On November 16, shortly after he arrived, Yardley was again reading messages coming in by telegraph, but this time the view from his window was not the flat Indiana countryside; it was the tennis court on the South Lawn of the White House. He was working as an $18.75-a-week code clerk for the State Department and had become a silent spectator of American diplomacy. But as he listened to the stuttering resonators and sounders on the oak telegraph table, he began to wonder how many other silent spectators might be copying and deciphering those same highly confidential missives; he knew it was a practice engaged in by other countries. Then it struck him: Why shouldn't the United States employ such "decipherers" to solve the secret codes and ciphers of others? "As I asked myself this question," he later wrote, "I knew that I had the answer ... to a purpose in life. I would devote my life to cryptography."

Yardley read the few works on the subject at the Library of Congress and began practicing on the State Department's own messages. To his amazement, he solved in less than two hours a coded, personal message sent to President Wilson by his special envoy, Colonel House. Convinced that if he could so easily solve American codes, other countries could too, he drew up a paper on the subject for his superior, David Salmon. Salmon was shocked and quickly came up with another code, but just as quickly Yardley was back with the solution.

With the outbreak of World War I, Yardley switched from State to the War Department where, on June 29, 1917, he organized Section Eight of Military Intelligence (MI-8), responsible for all code and cipher work within the division. This was the first link in the long genealogical chain that would eventually lead to the present National Security Agency.

Lieutenant, later Major, Yardley quickly proved the worth of the cipher organization, and by the time of the Armistice, on November 11, 1918, MI-8 had solved a total of 10,735 messages sent by foreign governments, a truly impressive accomplishment. At the time the war ended, Yardley was in Paris, trying to nudge a greater degree of cooperation out of the secret French Chambre Noire. It was decided that he should remain in the French capital to run a code bureau attached to the American Commission to the Peace Conference.

On April 18, 1919, Herbert Yardley returned to the United

States and began arguing for a peacetime continuation of the codebreaking activities of MI-8. He submitted a memorandum describing a Cipher Bureau, to consist of fifty cipher experts and clerks, with a budget of $100,000 and himself as chief. Within a few days both the State and War Departments agreed to fund jointly the secret organization, and on May 20 America's Black Chamber was born.

Housed in a four-story brownstone at 3 East 38th Street, under the cover of a commercial code company, the Black Chamber found its prime targets in the code and cipher systems of an increasingly aggressive Japan. Yardley promised to solve them within a year or resign. And in one of the most important achievements in American cryptologic history, Yardley succeeded, with months to spare.

Just how valuable Yardley's breakthrough was became abundantly clear during the 1921–1922 Washington Disarmament Conference. The goal of the five-nation conference was to set limits on the tonnage of warships sailing the world's oceans, and the chief objective of the State Department was to limit Japan to a ratio of 6 to 10, in favor of the United States. Although Japan was publicly insisting that the lowest it would go was a 7-to-10 ratio, Yardley's Black Chamber knew differently. Through the intercepted and deciphered Japanese messages passing between that country's negotiators, Yardley had learned of Tokyo's hole card: if necessary it would drop down to the 6-to-10 ratio. Following Yardley's advice, the State Department held tight, and, as the cipher chief predicted, Tokyo eventually threw in its hand.

With the end of the conference, on February 6, 1922, the Black Chamber began to die. Because of new laws guaranteeing the secrecy of communications, as well as because of policy disagreements between the federal government and Western Union, the Chamber's secret supply of telegrams was all but cut off. At the same time, with both the war and the disarmament conference receding from memory, the State Department started to cut back on Yardley's budget. This was especially serious, because it was from the State Department that the Black Chamber was now deriving the bulk of its financing.

By 1924 Yardley's budget had been slashed to a quarter of its original $100,000, the staff reduced to a meager seven, and the roomy town house abandoned for two small rooms in an office building at 52 Vanderbilt Avenue. Ironically, however, what eventually doomed the Black Chamber was not apathy, but moralistic outrage.

In March 1929 Herbert Hoover entered the White House and conservative Henry L. Stimson took over the State Department. Two months later the new Secretary of State discovered the Black Chamber and angrily denounced it with what no doubt has become the most famous quotation in the history of American cryptology: "Gentlemen do not read each other's mail." At midnight on October 31, 1929, the Black Chamber was permanently bolted shut.

For Yardley, things could not have looked darker. Not only was he out of work and experienced only in breaking foreign codes and ciphers, but the stock market had just crashed and the Great Depression was now underway. Packing his bags, he headed back home to Worthington. There was no more need for codebreakers in southwestern Indiana than there was in New York, though, and Yardley, broke and with a wife and son to feed, began to feel desperate. There was one thing he could do: he could write a book describing his exploits as chief of the Black Chamber.

Yardley's decision to write the account was not arrived at lightly. "Ever since the war I have consistently fought against disclosing anything about codes and ciphers," he once wrote to a friend. "My reason is obvious: it warns other governments of our skill and makes our work more difficult."

But, Yardley reasoned, the situation had now changed. America no longer had a Cipher Bureau, nor was it still engaged in codebreaking, so what was there to injure? In fact, he concluded, publication might even have the beneficial effect of forcing the State Department to reconsider its unwise decision to close the Black Chamber.

With the help of a New York literary agent, George T. Bye, Yardley began his career as an author. His story first appeared in three excerpts in the *Saturday Evening Post* during April and May 1931, and on June 1 *The American Black Chamber,* published by the Bobbs-Merrill Company, made its appearance. It was about to become one of the most controversial books in American literary history.

The public rushed to buy the book, and the critics gave it their blessing, one calling it "the most sensational contribution to the secret history of the war, as well as the immediate postwar period, which has yet been written by an American." More recently, the author and code expert David Kahn wrote, "I devoured it. It was one of the most thrilling books I have ever read."

In Washington, the administration coldly denied Yardley's story, but privately officials were outraged. They considered a legal prosecution, but rejected the idea when they were advised that it would be both compromising and embarrassing. Nor could they find a precedent that would give them an excuse to suppress the book.

Yardley became something of a celebrity and — at a time when author tours were not usual — he traveled the country, boasting of the Black Chamber's successes and warning of a bleak future without it. Then, as lecture bookings fell off, Yardley turned to a new project. He decided to tell the story of the Washington Disarmament Conference as only he could — including copies of the intercepted signal traffic between Tokyo and the Japanese negotiators in Washington. With the assistance of an amateur writer named Marie Stuart Klooz, Yardley produced the 970 pages of *Japanese Diplomatic Secrets: 1921–22* in two months.

Bobbs-Merrill, however, had been thoroughly scared. Not

only did they reject the book, but D. L. Chambers, the firm's president, notified the Attorney General that the new manuscript contained the text of many Japanese messages.

Now the State Department panicked. At State's instance, three officers from the War Department went to Worthington and demanded that Yardley return all official documents. He replied that he had none that "would injure the strength of the United States Government."

But the government did succeed when Yardley's agent delivered the manuscript to the Macmillan Company. Thomas E. Dewey, then Assistant U.S. Attorney in New York, enlisted the cooperation of George Brett, Macmillan's president, and on February 20, United States marshals took the manuscript from Macmillan.

It was not the first or the last time a publishing house would participate in suppressing its own book, but it was the first time in history that the federal government had confiscated a manuscript for security reasons. More than forty-six years later, parts of the *Japanese Diplomatic Secrets* remained classified.

To ensure that Yardley produced no more exposés, the State Department got Congress to pass a law making it a crime to publish any material that has been prepared in any official diplomatic code. And that law is still on the books.

None of this discouraged Yardley from his new career as an author. He turned from nonfiction with a sprinkling of fiction to fiction with a sprinkling of fact. In his 1934 effort, *The Blonde Countess,* the chief of a secret Washington bureau during World War I unmasks a beautiful German spy. "Mr. Yardley knows his spy stuff and can tell a good story," wrote the *Saturday Review of Literature.*

The Red Sun of Nippon was finished six months later. Again, the plot revolved around espionage and diplomatic intrigue as the love affair between a young State Department employee and a beautiful Chinese woman led to the uncovering of a Japanese plot to conquer Manchuria. In 1935 more success came with a movie sale. MGM — with Yardley as technical adviser — brought *The Blonde Countess* to the silver screen under the title *Rendezvous,* starring William Powell, Rosalind Russell, and Caesar Romero.

In 1936, the world was attacked by an outbreak of small troubles that often signal worse things ahead. Germany moved its troops into the demilitarized Rhineland; Franco launched his rebellion in Spain. "One cannot help feeling," President Franklin Roosevelt wrote his ambassador in France, "that the whole European panorama is fundamentally blacker than at any time in your lifetime or mine."

In the Orient, the Japanese empire was on the move. In 1937, its armies invaded China, and by the end of July, Peking and Tientsin had fallen. Then came the heavy bombing of Shanghai and the sack of Nanking. As the Chinese Nationalist leader, Chiang Kai-shek, withdrew his troops and transferred his capital to remote Chungking, the American people became more and more sympathetic with his cause. The President was sympathetic, too, but he was also wary of provoking Japanese retaliation, so the United States did no more than supply arms to the desperate Chinese.

Chiang, in the midst of a war that was quickly becoming increasingly technological, felt a pressing need for better intelligence; specifically, for better signals intelligence. He asked the Chinese embassy in Washington to see whether one of the most gifted — and most notorious — figures in the field, Herbert Yardley, once again would perform his magic on Japanese codes and ciphers.

By now Yardley was settled in Queens and feeling bored with life as a real estate speculator. His "cipher brain" sorely missed the challenge of coded messages, and his hands itched to work out their solutions. When he was approached by Major Hsiao, the Chinese assistant military attaché, with the offer to come to Chungking, Yardley could hardly contain his excitement. He did, however, hold it in well enough to get the Chinese to raise his salary to about $10,000 a year. In addition, Yardley asked Hsiao for another favor — permission to bring with him to China the beautiful woman with whom he had recently fallen in love, Edna Ramsaier.

Twenty years earlier, Yardley had met Edna when, just out of high school, she had arrived at the Black Chamber in New York, applying for her first job. It was only after several nervous passes that she decided to enter the forbidding brownstone. Now the former chief and his long-time assistant were very much in love. Despite the sentiment, however, Hsiao could not authorize Yardley to have anyone accompany him to China.

In September of 1938, after several months of secret conferences with Major Hsiao, Yardley slipped out of the country and arrived in China under the *nom de guerre* of Herbert Osborn, ostensibly an exporter of hides. His chief was the stern-faced General Tai Li, head of the Chinese Secret Service and a man greatly feared throughout China, as evidenced by his nicknames: "the Killer" and "the Generalissimo's Number One Hatchet Man." Almost never was Tai's real name mentioned. According to Yardley, the graduate of China's prestigious Whampoa Military Academy had at one time spent several months in Shanghai attempting to engineer the assassination of one of his foes, Wang Ching-wei.

The Chinese Black Chamber, as Yardley later called it, was overly decentralized and in utter disarray when he arrived. It was loosely headed by a mysterious Chinese official who had been working on intercept and codebreaking for about ten years, but whose connection with the activity was known only to one or two persons in the Chinese government, and perhaps was never revealed even to Yardley. Below him were five entirely separate organizations, comprising, in all, about 800 people, which Yardley first sought to combine into one single unit. It was his hope eventually to become the head of the massive new organization. The reorganization, however, would be slow and painstaking.

Nightlife in Chungking was considerably less than that to which Yardley had become accustomed. Although his hosts had provided him with a house, he could usually be seen hunched over a deck of cards at the Chungking Hostel, a government-run hotel for foreigners on official business. Here the fifty-year-old dealer in hides would drink, play poker, and swap bawdy stories with the few other Westerners still hanging on in wartime Chungking. One of his best friends was George Schwer, a former enlisted man in the U.S. Navy who had decided to remain in China and had opened a business in town.

Another close friend was a green, twenty-three-year-old stringer for *Time* magazine, fresh out of Harvard. Theodore H. White, later to become renowned for his books on American presidential elections, had arrived in Chungking about five months after Yardley. A Chinese history major, White had traveled to China on a fellowship and managed to talk himself into a job in Chiang Kai-shek's government as adviser to the Chinese Ministry of Information, a job, he later recalled in his book *In Search of History,* * in which his principal mission was to "manipulate American public opinion." He added, "The support of America against the Japanese was the government's one hope for survival; to sway the American press was critical. It was considered necessary to lie to it, to deceive it, to do anything to persuade America that the future of China and the United States ran together against Japan."

Quickly tiring of his life as a propagandist, White signed on with *Time.* Between dodging bombs and sending "mailers" back to New York, White would frequent the Chungking Hostel, where he often rubbed shoulders with Yardley, of whom he later wrote, with fondness:

*(New York: Harper & Row), 1978.

"Osborn" took a fancy to me. He was a man of broad humor and unrestrained enthusiasms, and among his enthusiasms were drink, gambling and women. He decided after we had become friends that he should teach me poker, which he did by letting me stand over his shoulder and watch him unfold his hands and sweep up the pots. He also felt I should be taught sex, and tried to persuade me to sample that experience by inviting some of the choicest ladies he knew to a banquet in his house. I would not learn; Boston was still strong in me. But he did teach me something more important than anything I have learned since from any official American adviser or wise man: how to behave in an air raid. Yardley's theory was that if a direct hit landed on you, nothing would save you. The chief danger of an air raid, he said, was splintered glass from windows. Thus, when one hears the siren, one should get a drink, lie down on a couch and put two pillows over oneself — one pillow over the eyes and the other over the groin. Splintered glass could hurt those vital organs, and if the eyes or the groin were injured, life was not worth living. It was good advice for any groundling in the age before atom bombs; and I took it. Yardley was excessively kind to me, as were so many older men in Chiang K'ai-shek's Chungking.

By the end of his first year, Yardley had become severely homesick. Long periods of heavy drinking were interspersed with brief periods of total abstinence. His health was deteriorating, and he had lost a considerable amount of weight. By now, rumors of his true identity and the nature of his work were becoming open secrets among the small fraternity of foreigners, which included the officers of the American gunboat U.S.S. *Tutuila.*

By the summer of 1939, the rumors had reached the ears of Major David D. Barrett, the assistant United States military attaché in Chungking. He began trying to establish contact with the elusive Mr. Osborn, but Yardley carefully avoided him. Finally, on September 13, 1939, Barrett sent a secret message to Colonel E. R. W. McCabe, head of Military Intelligence (G-2) at the War Department. "Can you tell me if Yardley (of the

'Black Chamber') has left America?" Barrett wrote, adding, "According to a reliable report he or another individual of his trade has been employed since about May 25 by the Nationalist Government."

Military Intelligence had kept close track of Yardley throughout the 1930s and had known all along of his work in China. Since Yardley was a free agent, and America at the time benignly supported the Chinese Nationalists in their struggle against Japan, it was felt best to let sleeping dogs lie and not inform the embassy officials in Chungking. But now the situation had changed, and the War Department was trying to decide whether to take advantage of the situation.

Five days later, McCabe sent off a message to Barrett, informing him that the rumor was fact and authorizing him to approach Yardley very discreetly and "inquire if results of his work can be made available to you." McCabe noted that "particular interest attaches to material pertaining to military subjects." By now America was regarding Japan with fear. Apprehension of war in the Pacific was increasing daily, and it was hoped that Yardley could serve as a shortcut to breaking the Japanese army code. The enormous consequences of a leak, however, led McCabe to advise the military attaché, "Be guarded in your radio messages about this matter even when in secret code." So Yardley's name was never again mentioned in any other communication between Barrett and McCabe.

Yardley had good reason for being cautious. His chief, General Tai, had warned him about having any contact with foreigners or even with Chinese outside his own section. He also knew he was constantly being watched. After Yardley had been in China for a while, he had asked for and been granted a certain amount of freedom — but associating with an employee of the American embassy would be looking for trouble. Therefore, it was more than five months before Barrett was able to meet Yardley.

Tai was curious about the American diplomat's frequent

overtures, and Yardley informed him that, as an American citizen, he would naturally have occasional contact with the American embassy. Now he felt free to meet with Barrett, even though the fact of the meeting would most surely be reported back to his Chinese superiors.

On Thursday, February 22, 1940, Barrett and a very nervous Herbert Osborn Yardley met for the first time. Yardley told Barrett that until recently he had very much wanted to leave China after the expiration of his contract on March 31, but now had decided to stay on under an oral contract, provided that suitable terms could be reached. He also said that chances were good that he would be placed in full control of the newly centralized "Black Chamber."

Yardley spoke of the strain he had been under all these months in Chungking and told Barrett of his hope of visiting the fronts at Hunan and Kwangai in a week or so. He also mentioned that he was trying to improve the interception of messages sent from inside Japanese lines by long wave.

Barrett, in a low voice, delicately brought up the subject of Yardley's secretly cooperating with the American government and supplying material dealing with Japanese military traffic. Yardley had felt all along that this was what Barrett wanted, and he seemed pleased that his suspicions had been confirmed. He told the attaché that he would be very happy to cooperate with the War Department and asked him to find out, as soon as possible, specifically what the department wanted.

Major Barrett hurried back to the embassy and sent off a one-and-a-half-page message to Colonel McCabe, describing the results of the meeting. In Washington it was agreed that the material most needed was copies of the field cryptographic systems employed by the Japanese army — if they could be obtained without compromise.

Remembering Yardley's lack of discretion once before, McCabe worried that the approach to him might backfire and damage American foreign relations. For that reason, he advised

Barrett to use extreme caution in any dealings with Yardley. "Maintain absolutely reserved but friendly relations with him without any commitment or encouragement which he might interpret as an approach to obtain his services," the colonel wrote. Hoping that Yardley's cooperation could be won simply by waving the flag, McCabe added: "If without solicitation and as a matter of patriotism he should offer you information especially concerning the cryptographic systems employed by units of the Japanese Army in the field you are authorized to accept it." Other information, Barrett was told, "is not desired."

On Friday, March 8, two weeks after the first meeting, Barrett again met Yardley and told him of G-2's response. Yardley said that he would try to get his new contract to stipulate that he be given complete records of all work done by his section. He added that his section had achieved definite success in breaking the Japanese military codes, and he explained that delivering the requested material would not only entail a great deal of hard work and the exercise of careful diplomacy, but would also involve considerable risk. Too much risk for patriotism alone, Yardley said, adding that he felt the patriots working in Washington for the government were certainly well paid, and he saw no reason why he should not be compensated for his services. In addition, he claimed that the material would be worth at least $100,000 to the American government.

In return for secretly delivering to Barrett at intervals "complete technical records all steps in busting Jap military codes," Yardley wanted nothing for himself, but insisted on an agreement whereby the government would find a position paying $6,000 a year for the woman he missed dearly, Edna Ramsaier. He argued that Edna had been his assistant in the Black Chamber and that her services were worth at least $2000; the remaining $4000, he told Barrett, could be considered compensation for his risk.

G-2 found Yardley's condition totally unacceptable. They had never been more than lukewarm over the idea of dealing with him in the first place, and now decided to give a flat no to his condition. The major reason for worry was the fear that on his return from China Yardley might once again become literary and leave all those involved with a large order of egg on their faces. More important, however, and an argument most likely made by the War Department's Signal Intelligence Service, was that the SIS had already solved Purple, Japan's most secret diplomatic crypto system, after several years of work, and if Yardley ever wrote about selling one of their codes to America, the Japanese would again completely overhaul their cryptographic system, and the work of almost a decade would be lost.

Ironically, on March 4, 1940, only four days before Yardley's meeting with Barrett, Edna had been hired to work in the SIS by its chief cryptologist, William F. Friedman, a bitter, long-time rival of Yardley. At the time, Friedman had no idea of her relationship with Yardley, and when he found out he was furious and eventually gave her her notice. But Edna went over his head, appealed the firing, and was reinstated. Having won her point, however, she decided instead to work for the Weather Service.

Yardley was greatly disappointed by the rejection of his proposal. He had hoped that it would be a possible lead-in to a position in the United States. Nevertheless, he was not yet ready to concede defeat, and when Major William Mayer, the U.S. military attaché, arrived for a visit from Peking, Yardley brought him up to date on the proposal he had made to Barrett, the assistant attaché. Then, to show his sincerity and his ability to produce, Yardley handed Mayer a memorandum he had drawn up for General Tai, describing the progress of his unit since his arrival. In the memorandum, Yardley had listed nineteen different Japanese systems the unit had broken. In the next paragraph he explained that some time before, he had instructed his students to write detailed reports showing exactly how each of the systems was broken. "These MMS will be invaluable for future reference," Yardley added in his memorandum.

Now, pointing to this paragraph, Yardley told Major Mayer that he would be willing to offer the War Department copies of those reports. Mayer, doubting that Yardley could actually produce all that he said he could, noted in a letter to Military Intelligence in Washington that even if he could, he might not be able to get away with it. "I am certain that he is under surveillance and believe that the Chinese would know of any transfer of data he might make," Mayer wrote. Washington agreed, and again Yardley was left without a buyer for his goods.

By now his contract was almost up, and he had to decide whether to remain in China or return to the United States and again face an uncertain future. Yardley, always looking for a better bargaining position, notified General Tai that he had been informed by Major Mayer of the War Department's urgent need for him in Washington. Later that day, Yardley went over to Mayer's office and told him he was hoping for better terms on a new contract and asked him to back up his story. The major told Yardley in no uncertain terms that the War Department had made no such offer and that, if asked, he would tell the truth.

Several days later, General Tai asked Mayer to come to his office. Stressing the great friendship between the two countries, Tai asked about his approach to Yardley regarding a return to the United States. He emphasized that Yardley's work was by no means complete, and said that they were eager to keep him in Chungking for at least another year. Mayer replied that the War Department had made no request for Yardley's return.

Delighted, Tai then advised the major that if any results were achieved from Yardley's work, arrangements might be made to turn the material over to him, Mayer, for use by the American government. An astonished Mayer told Tai that, though he had no instructions on the point from the War Department, he personally believed that the information would be most welcome. Tai said they could talk more about the deal later, when the material was in shape. He also told Mayer that he would prefer to keep the whole matter on a personal basis between the two of them and not make it an official arrangement between their respective governments.

Mayer, notifying Washington, questioned whether the general might have been fishing for money, although he tended to doubt it. Colonel J. A. Crane, in charge of the Military Attaché Section, decided to leave the matter up to Mayer, but advised him, "If he should voluntarily make any of the material available to you, of course you may accept it but with the clear understanding that it is not on a reciprocal or purchase basis."

By June, the question had become moot. Physically sick — he had lost almost forty pounds — and unable to work because of intensive bombings, Yardley decided he had had enough. On Saturday, July 13, 1940, he boarded a plane and bade farewell to China.

Yardley — now reunited with Edna in Washington — completed a brief assignment for the Signal Corps, which involved describing his solutions of the Japanese army crypto systems. He then went on to other codebreaking exploits in the employ of the Canadian government and its new signals intelligence operation, the Examination Unit. When, for various reasons, that assignment came to an end, Edna and Herbert returned to Washington.

Yardley ended his long career in breaking codes and turned instead to breaking eggs; he opened a restaurant on the corner of 13th and H Streets. The Rideau was less than a smashing success; as Edna Yardley said with a laugh many years later, "That man was not fit for a restaurant."

Throughout the rest of the war and into the 1950s Yardley, banished from the field he himself had helped found, undertook a variety of jobs, including one as a ration enforcement officer with the Office of Price Administration. In 1945, together with an old friend, Carl Grabo, he wrote another novel, *Crows Are Black Everywhere,* which concerned the adventures of a woman journalist in war-torn Chungking. Later he wrote *The Chinese Black Chamber,* dealing with his days as a codebreaker in China, but, fearing renewed action by the federal government, decided not to submit the manuscript for publication. In 1957 he did publish *The Education of a Poker Player,* an enormously successful book, still in print, that explains the mysteries of the card game to enthusiasts. Ted White, his old friend from China, has called it a "major contribution to the American folk culture" and "as important in the education of the young poker-players as a sex manual is to a college freshman."

On Thursday, August 7, 1958, nine months after the *Poker Player* was released, America's most famous cryptologist died of a stroke suffered eight days earlier. He was sixty-nine. Four days later he was buried with full military honors at Arlington National Cemetery. The *New York Times* in its obituary called Yardley "the father of cryptography in the United States," a title that in fact he shared with others. But through his MI-8 and Black Chamber, Yardley had firmly set in place the foundation on which today's enormous and vital National Security Agency rests. And through *The American Black Chamber,* he had brought American cryptology out of the closet once and for all.

CAST OF CHARACTERS

Ling Fan *Chinese Interpreter*
Shon Ging *Chinese Girl*
Ching Pu *Chinese Scholar*
Number One *The Hatchet Man*
Number Two *His Assistant*
George McKay *Eurasian*
Wang Ching-wei *Chinese Traitor*
Shiu Chen *His Concubine*
General Tseng *Chief of Sabotage*
Lao Tsai *Chinese Houseboy*
Yang *Chinese Merchant*
Lao Fong *Chinese Chauffeur*
Hu Yeh *Chinese Girl*
Chen Huan *Chinese Engineer*
Tsu Fu
   Chinese Translator of Japanese
Fen Tao *Chinese Chauffeur*
Marguerite
   Chinese Sing-Song Girl
Elaine *Chinese Demimondaine*
One-Armed Bandit
   Chinese Traitor

Dorothy *His White Mistress*
Wu Fou *Chinese Interpreter*
Lao Han *Chinese Houseboy*
Schwer
   American Businessman
Pop *German Expatriate*
Herr Weiner *German Adviser*
Zelda *Russian Jewess*
Stephanie *Russian Girl*
Ted White *American Newsman*
Maya *Polish Girl*
Gilbert *English Adviser*
Stoney *Irish Adviser*
Ping *Chinese Informant*
Crofton *English Code Clerk*
Emily Hahn
   American Journalist
Ing-ing *Chinese Child Slave*
Maria *German Girl*
German Refugee *Japanese Spy*
Dr. Turnipseed
   American Officer

THE CHINESE BLACK CHAMBER

· Chungking, China, November 1938

*I*T IS HARD TO BELIEVE that I am here at last, after nearly two months of travel. I came by way of Europe and under the name of Herbert Osborn to avoid recognition and possible assassination by the Japanese. Upon the publication of *The American Black Chamber,* with its revelation of Japanese intrigue, I became a marked man in the Orient, and the Chinese authorities who had engaged me to organize a Chinese Black Chamber therefore decided to smuggle me in.

At Hong Kong I was met by my interpreter, Ling Fan, who was well supplied with money and instructed to provide everything for my comfort. Some days of anxious waiting followed, in which I endeavored to gain face with my interpreter. My advance reputation is formidable and I have the difficult task of trying to live up to it. My resourcefulness was put to the test almost at once.

Ling and I were drinking Scotch in the Hong Kong Hotel cocktail room and watching the beautiful and well-dressed Chinese women in their long, colored silk gowns, some slit above the knee. I was about to put Ling a question about the charms of Chinese women, when he asked, a bit diffidently, "Adviser, is it really true that a white woman's breasts are red?"

When I didn't answer at once he explained, "That's what a returned Chinese student from Paris told me."

"Is that all he told you?" I asked.

"Well, no," he said with some hesitation. "He also told me

— I don't know what you call it in English — but he told me it was also red."

Clearly it was up to me to show myself all-wise and powerful. I promised Ling to procure him a look-see, and to that end we set out upon my first assignment, surely a curious one for the foreign adviser in ciphers and counterespionage for the government in Chungking.

Outside the hotel a taxi was discharging an English officer and a blonde in a low-cut evening gown. Ling eyed her, his mouth driveling. A tall black-whiskered Sikh policeman nearby kept a crippled Chinese beggar and two curious children from approaching too near. I pushed Ling into the taxi and directed the driver to go to the police station. Ling was somewhat perturbed at this but more fascinated by the operation of the taxi meter.

At the station I went in alone and put to the pompous, mustached English colonel in charge my question: "Where can I find a white whore in Hong Kong?"

The colonel puffed up like a toad, told me there was none such, and if there were, the authorities would jolly well chase her out. I knew he was either a fool or lying. However, there was nothing to do but go. One of his Irish subordinates followed me out and gave me the desired address. There were two white prostitutes, he said, in the city — French, and quite nice too.

The apartment, presided over by a fat and rouged madame, was on one of the hills overlooking the bay. I left Ling outside while the madame and I conducted preliminary negotiations in a stuffy drawing room over port and Scotch and soda. An attractive brunette and a pretty blonde appeared. I explained in inadequate French that I was on my way to interior China. One, or both for that matter, could do me a great favor. They smiled their willingness. Then I pulled a sheaf of Hong Kong one-hundred-dollar bills from my coat pocket. I could well afford to be generous, for Ling had given me $1000 Hong Kong when he met me at the boat — a little gift from my future boss, the Hatchet Man, with which to amuse myself while in Hong Kong. I extracted two bills and replaced the others.

I was too new in the Orient to be sure of the status of the yellow man among white prostitutes and so told my story, experimentally, about a friend of mine: he didn't wish to go to bed with them; merely wanted to see them *au naturel.* Would they undress before him?

They must have thought me crazy, for they looked at each other and laughed gustily. Then they wanted to know if I was the "friend."

I said, "No, he's my Chinese interpreter."

"Chinese?" they cried. Then venomously, "*Le chien!*"

"Not for two hundred Hong Kong?" I asked.

"*Le chien!*" they cried again and spat.

I found myself outside, lying to the expectant Ling. I succeeded in putting him off. But my responsibility was only deferred. Face must be saved, and the honorable adviser must be proved to be infallible.

2

Air service to Hankow was discontinued the day I arrived in Hong Kong, because the fall of Hankow was imminent. Also, the Japanese were closing in on Canton and pressing against Kowloon, British controlled. If the British were nervous, no less was I. It had been planned that I was to fly to meet "Our Leader," the Generalissimo, and thence to Changsha to set up espionage headquarters. Such had been the instructions of the Hatchet Man, god of China's Intelligence Service, whose name, like that of some tribal deities, is tabu. Because of Japanese landings and bombings, plans had to be changed. Ling at the Chinese undercover office got in radio communication with the Hatchet Man and announced that in three hours we were to sail for Haiphong in French Indo-China.

I was even more upset by this than by the prospect of being picked up by the police for registering under a false name, carrying concealed weapons, and possessing three suitcases filled with brochures on espionage, codes, and ciphers. The aggregate sentences for these offenses would doubtless exceed my life expectancy. To go by sea to Haiphong was to court destruction at the hands of Japanese naval vessels. If the Japanese should board our tramp steamer, as they were quite likely to do, my number would be up, false name and false passport notwithstanding.

Ling, however, came armed with the necessary forged documents for the attempt. There was a passport in the name of Herbert Osborn and a medical certificate to the effect that I had taken cholera and smallpox injections. The certificate had been predated ten days, a requirement for entering Indo-China. As a matter of fact, I had had such injections, whereas Ling has never had one in his life and intends not to have. But he runs, no doubt, a minor risk in wartime.

At dark we slipped aboard a freighter, and except for a few moments when a Japanese cruiser ordered us to heave to while they shelled Paloi, a small Chinese port, our voyage to Haiphong was uneventful. But those few moments were a lifetime to me, and I held my breath until the Japanese cruiser steamed away.

The Hatchet Man's undercover agent met us at Haiphong and bribed us through the customs. My phony passport was not challenged and now I could relax. There would be no difficulty at the Chinese border.

So it proved, though we waited three days before securing transportation on the biweekly narrow-gauge to Kunming, China. The all-powerful Hatchet Man had thoughtfully provided for our entertainment during our enforced wait. His agent led us to a taxi-dance dive and plied us with champagne, and there a pretty Annamite with blackened teeth danced divinely with me until 2:00 A.M.

The Hatchet Man's agent was instrumental in my saving face with Ling, whom I had disappointed in the affair of the French ladies in Hong Kong. Through him I called on a French manicurist-friend of the police commissioner. Surprisingly enough, she agreed to the proposal I made her, and Ling's curiosity was satisfied. As a consequence, I stand high in his eyes and am unquestionably destined to be a great man in China.

Again at Kunming, China, an undercover agent appeared and, though all seats to Chungking by plane were booked a month ahead, he secured us passage on a transport plane carrying a load of high-octane gas in five-gallon tins. The pilot, an American named Woods, a noted character in these parts, had been flying in China for six years. On our flight to Chungking, Woods turned his ship over to the co-pilot and talked with me for half an hour. He was very careful not to inquire my business, for which I was glad, not wishing to lie to him. The Orient is like the Old West in its avoidance of prying curiosity. Foreigners ask no personal questions of each other. What but necessity or some political or criminal activity would drive a white man like myself to Chungking? Woods, out of kindness, offered to have me put up on the American gunboat, for there was, he said, no place in Chungking. When I explained that I left all such matters to my interpreter, he said no more about it and changed the subject.

We flew above the clouds all the way to Chungking, and I saw nothing whatever of China until, miraculously, we came out of the clouds and landed upon a little sandy island in the middle of the Yangtze River. To the north, on its rugged promontory formed by the junction of the Little River and the Yangtze, sprawled the city of Chungking, a scurf of mud and bamboo huts and low, dull-colored stone buildings. I was depressed. It was a dreary prospect, which stirred in me dark premonitions of evil to come.

There was nothing to dispel this oppressive mood when we arrived in the city itself. A sampan ferried us to the foot of a cliff, and sedan chairs bore us up a flight of three hundred steps to the muddy streets at the top, where a car awaited us. A winding narrow highway flanked by lines of rickshas brought us past the western gate to a small four-story apartment building overlooking the Little River, which is the northern boundary of Chungking.

3

My office and a suite of living rooms are on the third floor. This, it seems, is a hideout of the Hatchet Man, who has one in every large city. Ling proudly displayed the bathroom, a rarity in this city of a million people, where there are not more than a half-dozen in all. A houseboy brought us hot towels and two glasses of scalding water. I was about to use my glass as a finger bowl, but caught myself when Ling wiped his face with the towel and drank the hot water. It was dangerous, Ling explained, to drink unboiled water, and all that could be had was from our long-spouted tea kettle. I said I preferred Scotch even without ice or cold water, and drank it so from the bottle.

Two undercover officials came to dinner, which we ate with chopsticks seated on stools about a round table. I was given the traditional seat of honor, facing the doorway. Thus, no enemy could creep up on me undetected. The dinner consisted of innumerable dishes, most of which I did not recognize. Throughout the meal, which, it seemed to me, lasted for hours, we toasted each other with small cups of hot yellow wine, turning the empty cups toward each other with each drink and saying *"kam-pei,"* which means dry cup. After a long bout of this, the yellow faces of the three Chinese turned red, and I felt none too happy.

"How long does this go on?" I finally demanded of Ling.

"As long as the honorable guest wishes."

"Well," I said, "the honorable guest wishes to go to bed. How the hell does he end it?"

"Just stand up," Ling said.

I contrived to do so, and the guests were equally successful.

They bowed, took their hats and coats, bowed a second time, and departed. There is something to be said for this Chinese custom. Guests make a clear break, like fighters in the ring. There are no long-drawn and wearisome farewells. But despite the wine I had drunk and the welcome departure of my guests, I went to bed apprehensive and dispirited. The apartment was cold with a cold that penetrated to the bone and that alcohol could not dispel for long. Outside my window lay the dark, crowded, fog-wrapped city housing a million yellow men whose ways were strange and whose thoughts were hidden from me. Chungking means Heavenly Residence, but I would have given a good deal to be in Worthington, Indiana, which was never so characterized.

The morning was no better, for the day was damp and chill, and my bones ached after a night spent upon a thin cotton mat spread on a hard bed of bamboo. There was no heat whatsoever, and even with my overcoat on I was cold. Ling was nowhere about and the chef had gone to the markets. The houseboys, misunderstanding my sign language, brought me, instead of food, a bottle of whiskey.

That cheered me a little, but I was hungry and I feared to leave the house, because I didn't know where I was. My failure to communicate my thoughts to the houseboys was absolute. I took a small map of Chungking from the wall, motioned them to follow, and pointed first to the map and then to the address in Chinese above the street door. The two guards stationed there joined in the game. Not one of them had the slightest inkling that I wished them to point out on the map the place of the apartment house.

Thereupon I drew the Chinese characters as best I could and set off down the street. The two guards ran after me, shook their heads, and motioned me back. I remained outside, smoking. When I flicked an unfinished cigarette into the street, a half-naked ricksha coolie snapped it up as a fish rises to a fly, scarcely breaking his stride. I lighted other cigarettes and tossed them into the street, making bets with myself. I had established a record of five seconds when the Number One houseboy called me inside and introduced me to a pretty Chinese girl in a blue cotton gown who curtsied and told me in broken English that she lived next door with an uncle and other relatives. She offered to have her *amah* prepare me breakfast or to poach some eggs herself in my servants' quarters on the top floor. Politely, I begged her not to bother. This was a mistake, because she did not repeat the offer. However, she marked the map for me, went with me to the street, and hailed an empty ricksha. Cautioning me to pay not more than thirty cents each way, she gave the coolie directions, and with my protesting guards jogging along behind, I was borne to a dirty teahouse on the edge of the city, where I breakfasted on tea and duck livers dipped in black pepper, the two guards sullenly watching the while.

I searched the street for a present to reward my benefactress but could find nothing but a bottle of cheap German perfume, the label faded. This I sent to the Chinese girl, with a note asking her to have dinner with Ling and me. She answered:

> Dear Mr. Osborn: I should say "very sorry" to you tonight. I have another party at home. Some time I like to have you for tea party. Thank you so large for your dear present. Good-bye.
>
> Lu Shon Ging

By the time of Ling's return, I had finished half the bottle of whiskey out of sheer boredom. He was angry because I had gone out alone. I assured him I had been careful and showed him my snub-nosed .25-caliber automatic, which, of course, he had often seen before.

"Oh that!" he said disgustedly.

As proof of its deadliness I shot a hole through the Hatchet Man's door, which made Ling angrier still.

No news from the Hatchet Man, absent on some mysterious mission; no sign of students or captured documents to decipher. However, a soft-spoken Chinese student newly returned from

II

Germany, Ching Pu, will translate some of my cipher brochures into Chinese. And to kill time I'm outlining an elementary course in cryptography, which Ching will also translate. He is an eminent Chinese scholar, speaks better English than Ling, and is wise in Western manners.

4

Ling and I have been to tea at Lu Shon Ging's, where I met two of her country cousins, who spoke no English and scarcely a word of Chinese. They were bashful, rose and stood at my entrance, and were wholly ill at ease, as was I. I cannot get used to the deference shown by Chinese girls to every male. Shon Ging, despite her education at a mission school, got up from her wicker chair when I offered her a cigarette, bowed, and thanked me, but refused to let me light it. Instead, she lighted mine.

The apartment was bare. There were no rugs, no curtains, no pictures or scrolls. This is China's war capital and no luxury city. For heat there was a huge iron pan of glowing charcoal, supported by a wooden base. A houseboy in a faded blue gown served us sweet cakes and tea without sugar.

In the evening the charming Shon Ging had dinner with Ling and me and a girl friend of Ling's at a bamboo teahouse overlooking the Little River. The girls were ill at ease, because the foreigner with his bald head was an object of curiosity. The Chinese diners stared at me, and I stared back at the men and women who slopped food on the tables, threw unwanted portions on the floor, and constantly rinsed their mouths with water, which they spat into convenient spittoons.

A round-eyed child of four sitting on its mother's lap began to cry and screamed something at me over and over. My three guests turned red beneath their yellow skins.

"What's it screaming?" I asked Shon Ging, who hung her head and would not answer.

"Let's hear it, Ling," I demanded.

Ling, too, was embarrassed.

"You must not feel bad, Adviser. The child calls you *'yang-kueh.'* "

"*Yang-kueh,*" I repeated. "That doesn't sound too terrible."

"It means foreign devil," said Ling.

"Well, aren't we?" I asked.

"You are in interior China," Ling explained. "To frighten children to be good, mothers say foreign devil will get them. Mothers tell their children that foreign devils have horns, blue eyes, a big nose, and red hair." He laughed. "You don't fit the description."

Even Shon Ging, with a glance at my bald head, laughed at this.

After dinner Ling took his friend home on a dilapidated bus run on vegetable oil and alcohol. Shon Ging insisted that I go with Ling, saying that she would walk home alone. I insisted that it was too dangerous, and followed by my two guards, we started out. At a muddy spot in the road a number of ricksha coolies lay sprawled on the sidewalk, and when I took her arm to guide her, they laughed and said something that made her tremble.

She was silent all the way home. At her door she said, "You are honorable foreign adviser. Much respected in China. I want you should study Chinese customs."

This and her trembling at the coolies' remarks puzzled me. When Ling returned, I asked him about it. But he pretended not to know, so the next day I questioned Ching Pu, the Chinese scholar who is translating my works. He told me that ignorant Chinese, and even most of the educated, sneer at a Chinese woman seen alone with foreign men.

" 'East is East and West is West,' " Ching quoted sadly. "In America, also, women lose face if seen alone with a Chinese gentleman. It is no different here." He smiled. "And I must also tell you no Chinese gentleman would take a woman's arm in public."

"But that's because you make Chinese women walk behind you," I protested.

"That is Chinese custom," he said gravely.

"I meant no offense," I said. "But you haven't told me what the coolies said. I know they called me *yang-kueh,* foreign devil. But even the child at dinner called me that. What else did they call me?"

He reflected a long while before answering.

"I will tell you," he said, "only that you will understand never to ask a Chinese girl of good family to accompany you unescorted. Ling Fan should have told you. The Chinese coolies did not call you anything. They spoke to the girl. They asked her, '*Yang-kueh tse ti kuei-t'ou pi chiao wu-men chung-kuo-jen-ti ta ma?*' "

I waited for him to translate.

"That means something like this," he said. " 'Do foreign devils have bigger turtle-heads than we Chinese boys?' "

• *Chungking, December 1938*

WE HAVE MOVED to a tile-roofed chateau built of stone blocks stolen from Buddhist temple ruins. It is situated high on the Chungking promontory overlooking the muddy waters of the Yangtze and the airfield where I landed on my arrival. Still higher to the northwest is the Russian embassy, and to the east, but five hundred yards distant, are the German, French, and English embassies. For three miles beyond these, the city sprawls to the confluence of the Yangtze and Little River. Beyond the Yangtze to the south rise low mountain ranges sheathed with pines and crested with pagodas.

My chateau was, I am told, the home of Chungking's mayor, who was mysteriously and quickly dispossessed just before my coming. There are some twenty rooms, pine-floored and with unpainted plastered walls. But for a few pieces of cheap furniture the rooms are bare. The windows are without blinds or curtains. There are no bathrooms, fireplaces, or stoves, except for the earthen charcoal ranges in the basement used for cooking. I have my bedroom and sitting room on the top floor of the east wing. For furniture I have a Western bed with a thin cotton mat in lieu of springs, a washstand with bowl and pitcher, a few chairs, a settee, and a commode. Though there is electricity, the lines are so overtaxed that even a 200-watt light is dim.

Beneath the chateau is a cave chiseled from the solid rock, where, Ling says, the Buddhist monks of ancient times secreted young girls. Ling, I fear, has a depraved mind. Today the cave is a bomb-proof dugout where candles burn night and day in anticipation of Japanese bombings, which are expected at any moment. For Chungking is the new capital and awaits hordes of downriver refugees, together with large numbers of government officials and employees. Throughout the city, day and night, are to be heard the ring of steel hammers and muffled explosions, as coolies blast other caves from the bowels of Chungking.

To reach the chateau from the city you take a narrow, muddy side street that branches from the main thoroughfare above the river, pass for half a mile through stinking bamboo slums, and at the dead end climb steps through a stone arch mounted with lions to an old ruined Buddhist temple and on to a stone wall with barred wooden gate on which are written Chinese characters meaning Pleasant Home. You ring a bell by pulling a cord. A Chinese guard looks through a shutter and takes down the bars. You then climb stone steps to a garden with stone walks and stone tea tables, shaded by palms and hedges. You pass a spring whose arch says "Sweet Water" and then, after a climb of forty steps, you come to the entrance of the chateau itself.

2

Chungking is in about the latitude of Cairo, Egypt, but its winter climate is chill because of the thick fogs that descend from China's snow mountains to the west and obliterate the sun. These same fogs are the protection of Chungking from bombing raids for part of the year. With the coming of warm weather, when the fogs are dissipated, it will be a different story. I could almost welcome the change, or so I fatuously think now, for I shiver and shake and daily drink a gallon of hot orange juice spiked with yellow wine to warm my marrow. The orange squeezer, unheard of by Chungking natives, is a handmade affair of my own design. Ling promises me an iron charcoal pan, but he is a congenital optimist and pleasant liar. Things move slowly here, I perceive, and I fret at my inactivity.

Ling and I are alone but for an army of guards and servants. Word comes from the Hatchet Man that the chateau is to be my workshop and the living quarters of my students, who are now, Ling says, coming by truck from Changsha. I hope they were out of the city before it was burned, for the military commander, believing the Japanese to be approaching, set fire to it, trapping two thousand unfortunates, who were burned to death. The rumor of the Japanese advance proved to be false. So the Generalissimo has ordered that the three top culprits be beheaded.

Perhaps my students have escaped the fire in Changsha, because there is a great deal of activity — installing desks, tables, blackboards, stationery, Chinese writing brushes and pencils, bamboo cots, and the like. Word has come, too, that a truckload of canned foreign food bought for me in Hong Kong, and an automobile, have landed on the South China coast and are headed northward. Well, we shall see.

The place is infested with rats. The rats of Szechuan, Ling boasts, are the largest and fiercest in China. Only a few days ago a rat killed the newborn baby of one of our guards, tearing out his testes before the mother could interfere. Despite traps set at my insistence, rats gallop in the attic, and scarcely a night passes that I am not awakened by one or two running over me. Though I have had the holes to my quarters plugged, there is a secret entrance I can't find. Sometimes before retiring, Ling and I turn out the lights and at the first rustle snap them on, but so far without discovering the rats' entrance. There is the one compensation that if you stay up half the night fighting rats, you sleep longer in the morning. I can work only eight hours a day on cipher scripts, for the work is close and tiring. As I have no amusements, time hangs heavy on my hands.

My boredom is lightened occasionally in the absence of Ling, who disapproves, by a visit from Lu Shon Ging. She is teaching me a few words of conversational Chinese and promises to find me an English-Chinese book to study between visits. Today she wore a silk gown and furs and looked very pretty. I think her English is improving with practice.

China's Black Chamber may soon become a reality, because yesterday I had a wireless from the Hatchet Man. Translated, it reads:

> Honorable Adviser: Your coming to China is highly appreciated. I would come up to Chungking to meet you were I not preoccupied with military affairs, which I regret. Now that you are living in Chungking I am concerned to know whether food and quarters are suitable. The Generalissimo is directing operations at the front and will not be able to come up to Chungking for the time being. But when he does come, I will take you to see him.
>
> With cordial regards, etc., etc.

To this I replied:

> Thanks so much for your kind telegram. I am very proud to be in China and shall do all in my power to make my mission a successful one. I am very happy in my living quarters and the food is excellent. I am of course looking forward to meeting you personally but quite understand that this is impossible now because of the military situation.
>
> With highest personal regards, etc., etc.

3

I have spent the day examining a number of captured documents brought from downriver by one of the Hatchet Man's henchmen and my immediate superior. Since the names are tabu, Ling has dubbed the Hatchet Man Number One and my superior Number Two.

Number Two, a general who has never smelled gunpowder, dresses in a khaki uniform with high collar and long trousers, leather shoulder strap and belt, and on the left side a sheath with a short sword. He is possibly thirty-five years of age. He has long ears, like most Chinese, and a round moon face. Though I am myself round-faced, I fear he is none too intelligent.

Ling introduced me with much ceremony, and after the usual

polite inquiries, I told him, Ling translating, what I would require in the way of radio equipment for interception of Japanese messages, direction finders to locate enemy stations, books, maps, and dictionaries for the research department. Also, I told him that I must have daily battle reports so that we can familiarize ourselves with place names of mountains, rivers, and towns; and the Japanese and Chinese armies' corps and division names, as well as their commanders. He should, I told him, delegate one man from Headquarters to keep a battle map up to date.

He made notes and, after a long flattering speech, rose to go.

"The general has instructed me to place all facilities at your disposal," he said.

I said, "My greatest wish right now is for captured documents."

"I had almost forgotten," he answered. "I brought a few with me from Hankow."

When his servant had procured them for me, I examined them eagerly. It was valuable material, especially so if prisoners had been taken who could facilitate its interpretation. Prisoners do not always talk, and Japanese prisoners were especially likely to be difficult, but I had come prepared for this. I had brought with me scopolamine and also sodium amytol, a harmless drug successfully used in the Crime Detection Bureau at Northwestern University. In America its involuntary use on criminals is illegal, but in China the Hatchet Man would, I was sure, impose no difficulties.

"You must," I said, "send a messenger at once and bring to Chungking all prisoners captured with these documents."

Ling translated, and Number Two stared stupidly at me. Ling's lips curled in a contemptuous sneer as he translated the reply: "The general says that will be impossible. The prisoners have all been executed."

· Chungking, December 1938

LING HAS AT LAST FOUND me a charcoal pan, which takes some of the chill from the sitting room I use as an office. But not before I caught the most severe cold of my life. My sinuses are running heavy pus, and for a week I have gradually been losing the sight of my right eye. Each night I place my bedroom clock under a light, and each night I must move closer to read the numbers on its face. Also, the drab blue gowns worn by the servants as seen through my right eye turn to purple, with flashes of red, and the blank spot in the center of all objects grows larger. Seven different Chinese downriver doctors, all educated abroad — some in America and England, others in Japan and Germany — have examined the eye. All but one tell me the optic nerve is injured. The seventh stands his ground and declares I have irido-cyclitis, a blood clot over the retina caused by an infection somewhere in the body. This infection, he says, may be caused by tuberculosis, syphilis, gonorrhea, teeth, tonsils, or what have you. I've had two syphilis tests, which were negative, an X ray taken at a mission hospital, also negative, and I have no signs of gonorrhea or other infection. My doctor is cheerfully unimpressed by this reassuring evidence. It seems I may have incipient tuberculosis of any part of the body, and this, though sufficient to cause irido-cyclitis, would not have been detected by the X ray. I am reminded of the incident in Cellini's *Memoirs,* in which, finding the glittering particle on his salad plate, he knew an attempt had been made to murder him. If the crystal was from a powdered diamond, his number was up. If glass had been substituted by the assassin and the diamond converted to cash, he would probably survive. But he had to wait a considerable time to find out — and meantime there was nothing to do but brood upon his symptoms. I've resolved to have my sinuses treated and, if that doesn't do the trick, to take an airplane to Hong Kong. The Chinese National Air Corps now makes a trip each night over the Japanese lines.

Neither refugees fleeing the Japanese nor my prospective students have yet arrived, but an army of generals with their families, servants, and concubines is upon us. Here, as everywhere in the world, generals and their possessions command the means of transportation, however many others may surrender to the enemy and die at his hands. My car hasn't yet arrived, but the sight of these many cars filled with Chinese officers made me angry. I demanded of Ling that he get one for me. As a result, I had one for two days. Yesterday it didn't show up. It is allegedly being "repaired."

There are no rickshas on this dead-end street, and I must wade in mud to the main road. I have no overshoes or boots, and Chinese sizes are too small for me. Last night on the way to a movie I blew up, much to Ling's admiration. He hopes someday to be a military attaché in Washington and assiduously studies all American expressions. He got an earful last night. Possibly not since Jackson's administration has so much rural profanity been packed in so small a compass. Ling's American vocabulary will have a distinctly Hoosier flavor. Among the characterizations that I asked Ling to pass on to Number Two was my opinion of the fat generals who stole my car and what he should do with the yellow bastards. Maybe something will come of it. Unless I throw my weight around a bit, I'll not get all the needed facilities and tools for my work. The car in itself is of minor importance.

I've been downtown several times, always followed by my

two guards, even though I go armed and can take care of myself. Ling dares not call them off, for besides the possible danger of my assassination by the Japanese, there are, he says, daily murders, kidnappings, and robberies. I trust the Hatchet Man will clean up the city when he arrives.

Though I can get a sedan chair or ricksha from the main thoroughfare to the center of town for twenty cents Chinese, which is three cents in American money, I often walk, since the distance is only a couple of miles. The streets are narrow and lined on each side with rickshas, so automobiles can barely pass each other. The business buildings are of dark brick or stone and none more than four stories high. The sidewalks, filled with Chinese in rags or long faded gowns, are brightened here and there by uniformed officers or prosperous civilians in new black or blue Chinese dress, followed by their wives or concubines clad in silk and furs. A foreigner is a curiosity and the cynosure of grinning Chinese when he stops to look in a store window or to light a cigarette.

At street stands are to be purchased — at ruinous prices in terms of Chinese currency — handmade combs, toothbrushes, fly swatters, bags of Chinese candy, peanuts, and watermelon seeds. The most fascinating article to me is a thin stick with a cotton tickler at one end, used to clean gum from the ears. Pig and water buffalo carcasses hang outside meat shops, which are furnished also with cured ducks, ancient eggs, soy-bean curd, and other delicacies. Street dentists operating with crude hammer, chisel, and pliers have the morbid attraction of a torture exhibit in a museum. And then there is the professional letter writer composing with swift strokes his mysterious pictographs for illiterate clients.

There are three Chinese cinema houses, all equally bad. Downstairs the price is fifty cents; in the balcony, eighty cents. For face, Ling buys balcony seats, which, besides, afford a better view of the rats racing in the aisles and on the stage. The American slapstick comedies at which the Chinese laugh and yell with delight have Chinese subtitles so that the action can be better understood. The news pictures are two years old. The last I have seen showed the coronation of King George of England and the burial of ex-President Taft.

I have a curious sense of isolation, living amid this torrent of exotic life whose ways and speech are strange to me. I am overwhelmed to think that in this vast country there are over four hundred and fifty million human beings — a fifth or more of the entire human race. Millions have died of flood or famine. Their loss will scarcely be noticed. A few fecund years, and the gaps are filled. In Western lands, with their flattening population curves, the so-called Malthusian law is merely a theoretical possibility. In Asia — in India and China, with their ancestor worship and their belief that every man must beget boy babies — it is a pressing and terrible fact. What will happen to the rest of the world when these countries are industrialized and become even more populous? If the dam breaks and the yellow waters overflow the earth, the so-called Yellow Peril will be just that. Happily, they are peaceful peoples, not prone to conquest. And but for their ancestor worship and their fertility cults, they are intelligent and educable. The race will be between education on the one hand and old customs and superstitions on the other. But to educate four hundred and fifty million in China and three hundred and fifty million in India is a stupendous, almost insuperable, task. Who is to do it and how?

2

Though I am closely guarded, I managed the other night to slip out of a movie house while a broken film was being repaired and the place was in darkness. I wandered to a teahouse, where I met a Eurasian man who speaks good English. His name is George McKay, and though his skin is yellow, he looks Irish and is an English subject, or so he says. He invited me to his charcoal-heated apartment, a sitting room and bedroom on the third floor of a compound in the heart of the city called the

German House. He leases the entire building and lets out the first floor for offices and the second and third floors as apartments.

At the entrance we encountered one of his tenants, a young Chinese lady expensively dressed, who acknowledged his introduction in perfect English. She joined us in his apartment and, after we were served the usual tea and cakes, accompanied us on the piano while we sang American and English songs.

She is small, warm, and engaging, a Eurasian, I imagine, for the bridge of her nose isn't flat like that of most Chinese. Her name is Shiu Chen. I asked, "What does Shiu Chen mean?"

She smiled and answered, "Shiu Chen means Fidelity."

After she had gone George peered into the hall and bedroom and then asked in a low voice, "Do you know Wang Ching-wei?"

"I only know of him," I replied. "I've heard him on the Chinese radio. He's China's silver-tongued orator, isn't he, and the Generalissimo's most hated rival?"

"They are bitter enemies," George agreed. "Wang dreams of ruling China. And he has powerful interests backing him."

"I'd like to meet him," I said.

"Wang trusts me," George replied. "I knew him well in Shanghai."

He looked around furtively and came close. "Shiu Chen is his favorite concubine."

And you're the paid watchdog, I thought. I didn't say that I knew Wang Ching-wei carried two bullets in his chest, fired, it is rumored, by assassins friendly to the Generalissimo. Was the Hatchet Man behind this, testing me out? I'd best watch my step.

"Favorite concubine," I said. "How many has he?"

He grinned. "Ten. It's no secret. Wang is very wealthy."

And a lucky dog, I reflected, as I plodded home through the mud.

Ling, who met me at the gate, was very angry indeed. I said

I had been bored with being cooped up with him every day and had slipped off to enjoy a little freedom. I spun him a tale of meeting a pretty Chinese girl who spoke English and of losing track of time.

"You worry me, Adviser," he said and looked so distressed that I laughed.

"There's no cause for worry," I answered him. "Her name is Fidelity."

· Chungking, December 1938

A CHINESE NOSE SPECIALIST, educated in Germany, whose surgical skill is about on a par with that of native dentists plying their trade on Chungking streets, dug into my sinuses and drained them with a suction pump. Primitive, but the oculist who examines me daily now has hopes for the eye.

Ling, much concerned about my health, bought a small electric heater for me, but when we hooked it up, all the fuses blew out. Two electricians then strung special wires from the transformer in the street. The heater thereupon gave forth a faint glow, at which the electricians grinned and shook their heads. I find that it requires 240 volts, more juice than the line carries.

Ling then searched the town for a stove but came back empty-handed. I told him about the "Message to Garcia." His simple Chinese mind, unconditioned to the techniques of advertising, was not impressed. So I told him to come along and we'd have a stove if I had to construct it myself. We first visited a junk shop, thence to a shop where copper utensils are made by hand, from this to a small blacksmith who makes iron cooking utensils, and finally to a larger forge down one of those steep alleys that drop to the river front. The owner shook his head until I drew a picture of what I wanted. He then agreed to make me, for a fabulous price, a special mold and pour me a cast-iron stove no larger than a two-gallon Texas hat and fitted with twenty feet of three-inch galvanized pipe. A few days later coolies set it up in my living room and ran the pipe out the window. It burns charcoal. The damned thing smokes but, with careful nursing, has dried out the room.

This morning Ling called me from my desk to the veranda. Below in my garden path two puffing coolies approached, bearing on their naked and calloused shoulders a gorgeous hand-carved sedan chair. This, with the aid of two others, they painfully lowered to the ground at the head of the steps. I thought it must be the Hatchet Man, but instead, out stepped a round-bellied Chinese general.

"It's General Tseng," Ling breathlessly announced a few minutes later. "Chief of sabotage."

I was delighted. Ever since my arrival I'd been urging Ling to send an officer to see me who knew about sabotage. Something could be done, I was sure, to cripple Japanese communications in occupied China and possibly to blow up munition plants and Yangtze cargo vessels.

"We'll go downstairs to the reception room," Ling suggested. The two flights of stairs to my quarters would prove quite too much for the chief of sabotage, I imagined.

In the reception room the fat general heaved himself erect from a bamboo chair and bowed politely. Lao Tsai, my Number One houseboy, set glasses before us on a bench, poured us boiling water from a long-spouted kettle, and handed us each a hot towel. The general wiped his shining round face and drank his scalding glass of water without turning a hair. He must have a tongue and gullet of alligator hide.

We exchanged amenities and he inquired about my health, my living quarters, and especially my food.

"Tell the general everything is quite all right," I said, though I sat shivering in the unheated room and could scarcely see him through my right eye.

His black eyes flickered slightly when I said I would like to talk with him of sabotage and saboteurs. Knowing it would be useless to ask him what was already being done, I drew diagrams of incendiary pencils, demolition sticks, and the like. The pencils, I could see, interested him most.

"They can safely be carried by spies," I told him. "They look exactly like real pencils. In fact, any pencil will do. You can steam it in two, bore out the two halves, insert incendiary glass tubes, and glue the two halves together again. To ignite it, you merely break off the point. This lets air into a glass tube, releasing a chemical that, when it eats through a thin copper shield, unites with a second chemical to engender a fierce white flame."

Ling and the general discussed this at considerable length. Finally Ling said to me, "General Tseng asks how the incendiary pencil is timed. How long after you break the point does it make a flame?"

"You do the timing when you make the pencil," I said. "For a short time, you make a thin copper shield so that the chemical eats its way through quickly; for a longer time, you make a thicker shield."

The general was much interested in all this and asked to know more. I told him that during the World War our enemies employed many saboteurs. In one case a saboteur working in a munitions plant in Kingston, New Jersey, caused a $5 million explosion. He worked in the plant, polishing 12-inch shells. One day he concealed an incendiary pencil in his coat, broke the point, and quickly walked away, leaving his coat behind. In a few moments his coat burst into a white flame. The employees ran, and when the fire reached the explosives, the plant went up in smoke and flame.

While Ling was translating this, I ransacked my memory for other spectacular instances and recalled the famous Black Tom explosion in Hoboken. This, too, was caused by incendiaries — a $20 million dollar job. It was started by saboteurs who crossed the Hudson River in a boat and landed secretly at a munitions dump along the shore. The explosion rocked the Jersey coast and New York City. Windows were shattered thirty miles away.

I wished to impress the general and so told Ling to get my copy of *The American Black Chamber,* which I had written in 1931. I turned to the picture of the German naval spy Pablo

Waberski, credited with engineering the Black Tom explosion and condemned to death through an intercepted cipher document I had unraveled.

The general nodded approval — at the explosions, I surmised, rather than at the capture of the spy.

"Also," I continued, "many ships were destroyed by incendiaries and by explosives made to resemble chunks of coal. These were concealed in piles of coal in the yards and later reached the bunkers of ships. There, they were shoveled by the stokers into the ships' fires, with results that can be imagined. The high explosive used is tetra. The effect is devastating."

Ling and the general went into a huddle.

"General Tseng says all Japanese supplies and munitions come up the Yangtze River from the east coast. The boats were seized from us and are loaded and unloaded by Chinese coolies. Thus, it would be easy for spies in occupied China to conceal your incendiaries and explosive in cargo or in coal. General Tseng wants to blow up these ships. He will send a chemist to consult with you. Meanwhile, you will please draw up a list of what is needed."

"Where will he get the stuff?" I asked.

"He will have it smuggled in from Hong Kong."

"By air, I hope."

"General Tseng says yes, by air."

"I have a question, Ling. Ask the general if these boats carry Chinese passengers as well as Japanese cargo and munitions."

Ling put his question, at which the general smiled cynically and responded in a single sentence.

"General Tseng says yes, the boats carry Chinese passengers, but that makes no difference."

2

Last night during dinner in a downtown restaurant I slipped away and left Ling and General Tseng's chemist deep in conversation. The foreign sounds beat against my ears and drive me frantic. Few of them have meaning for me — only the clatter of dishes, the barking of dogs, and the cries of children. The rest is merely noise, and at the end of a hard day it is more than I can bear. The Chinese must have strong nerves. They celebrate with tom-toms, gongs, and firecrackers. Like children, they apparently like noise for its own sake. And it seems that they must be insensitive to evil smells. How else can they endure the intolerable stinks of a city like Chungking? Barges laden with human excrement to be used as fertilizer in the fields pass nightly up the Little River. When the wind is from the north or west, the nauseating stink settles like a cloud upon the city.

In escaping from the dinner, I boldly passed my guards on the stairs on the pretext of seeking the toilet on the second floor, a primitive affair with a urinal and two foot stones on a veranda overlooking a malodorous alley. A Chinese wash adorned the veranda, and I cut the bamboo fiber line on which this was hung, fastened it securely, and swung myself to the ground.

George McKay was not at home, but his houseboy let me in and served me tea. I was playing cracked records on the gramophone when someone knocked. I unlocked the door. There stood Fidelity, smiling and even more charming, I thought, than before. It was good to speak English again and to dance with a woman for a few moments, even to the music of cracked records.

"I must go back," she said when she had finished her tea. "The men are in my apartment gambling."

"Poker?" I asked.

"*Mah-jong.*"

"Men don't want women around when they are gambling."

"It's really a party. Other women are there." She hesitated. "You knew that I'm Wang Ching-wei's concubine, didn't you?"

"No," I lied. "I didn't know that. I'd like to meet your husband. I've heard much of him."

"I wouldn't if I were you," she said and frowned.

I wondered why she would say that.

"I wasn't merely being polite," I returned. "I really want to meet him."

"Perhaps when George comes," she conceded reluctantly. "I must go now."

When George showed up an hour later I put it up to him. "I'll see what I can do," he said and left.

Shortly he returned, accompanied by Fidelity and a Chinese gentleman in foreign dress, white collar, and black tie. She introduced him in Chinese, and he, without bowing, extended his hand and smiled pleasantly. He had the broad nose and large nostrils of the Cantonese, but the bridge was more prominent than in most. His hair, cut long in the foreign style, was combed straight back. I find it difficult to judge the age of the Chinese, but I judged Wang to be in his early fifties.

Though I was under the impression that he both understood and spoke English, he said politely in French that he was always happy to meet Americans and hoped I would like China. He did not ask my business here, but I am sure he knows who I am. Would there be a war in Europe? he asked. I said yes. Would America help China in her struggle against Japan?

"With money, perhaps," I said.

A few days before, the Japanese premier, Prince Konoye, had presented peace terms that, if accepted, would reduce China to a puppet state. I wanted to ask him whether China would consider such terms, for rumor had it that Wang, as leader of the peace party, was urging acceptance. But I had sufficient sense to hold my tongue.

As he left to resume his game, I said, "I hope you win."

"I never win at *mah-jong,*" he said with a laugh, and as he departed, accompanied by the charming Fidelity, I thought of the old adage "Unlucky at cards . . ."

3

It was raining hard when I left George's house. My dead-end street is too steep for rickshas, and I waited for an empty sedan chair. "Shen Shien Tung Gai," I shouted at two dripping coolies. They stopped and gazed at me blankly. I repeated the name of my street, but they only shook their heads. Then I gave them a slip of paper with my address written on it. They couldn't read. A passing Chinese gentleman looked at my slip and said, "Shen Shien Tung Gai," at which they laughed understandingly. It sounded the same to me, but the meaning in Chinese depends so largely on pitch and inflection that I must have said something wholly meaningless to their ears.

They carried me through the driving rain to the fork leading to my place. There they stopped and swung the chair to the ground. I got out and pointed up my road, but they merely shook their heads, held out their hands, and jabbered unintelligibly. I paid, cursed them soundly, and, wet to the skin, plodded up my street, ankle-deep in mud.

I thought cheerfully of the hot bath awaiting me at home. Heretofore Ling and I had gone for baths to a downtown compound, where we could get a charcoal-heated bedroom and a hot bath, unless the whole place was already booked by the generals and their concubines. But now I had my own private bath. The small room adjoining my bedroom had been converted by wireless command of the Hatchet Man into a bathroom. The bathtub, toilet, and wash basin were molded locally from cement and small white pebbles, and the fixtures flown in from Hong Kong. The sewer pipe ran through the garden wall, where the sewage was collected by coolies and sold at the wharves for fertilizer. From the Yangtze, five hundred steps below, coolies carried my bath water in huge wooden buckets suspended at either end of a bamboo pole balanced upon their shoulders. This they poured into a wooden tank below my window and pumped by hand to another tank on the roof. There it fed by gravity through pipes into the bathroom. The job had been completed only late that afternoon.

"You can have a hot bath tonight," Ling had told me before we went to dinner.

"Hot bath?" I asked. "That river water is like ice."

"Half river water, half boiling water from the cooking ranges. Just leave it to Lao Tsai."

At the gate, drenched and muddy, I rang the gate bell in anticipation of the promised bath. Upstairs, I found Lao Tsai poking at my two-gallon stove. He always contrives to be busy when I arrive.

"Mr. Ling no come," he informed me.

The unfortunate Ling was no doubt still searching for me. I began to take off my shoes. Lao Tsai offered to help.

"Never mind," I told him. "I can manage. Just bring me a bottle of whiskey and fix me a hot bath." He didn't understand. "Whiskey, hot bath," I said. When you simplify the English language the Chinese catch on.

He poured me a sizable drink and just stood there, not making a move.

"Hot bath," I yelled, shivering despite the whiskey. "Hot bath! Savvy?"

"Me savvy, Adviser. Me sorry. No bath."

"What the hell are you talking about?" I demanded, forgetting that he understood only pidgin English. "No bath? Why?"

"No water no bath," said Lao Tsai.

I dragged him to the bathroom. Pointing to the roof I said, "Plenty water."

"Plenty water there" — he grinned — "no water here."

I opened the tap to the bathtub and swore.

"Pipe — he constipated," Lao Tsai offered cheerfully.

"God help me," I muttered, took another drink, and crawled beneath the covers. To escape Ling's anger, I feigned sleep when he returned.

• Chungking, January 1939

I WAS AT MY DESK, bathing my right eye in hot water, and Ling was translating the day's afternoon sheet hopefully called a newspaper, when the Hatchet Man came in, unannounced and accompanied by Number Two.

"It's Number One!" Ling whispered.

I rose, and the Hatchet Man bowed while Ling performed the customary elaborate introduction. He was dressed in the blue-black high-collared uniform of the party. Perhaps forty, gimlet-eyed, and of medium stature, he wore his unruly hair cut foreign style and parted at the side. He carried himself with the air of one who has power and uses it intelligently and ruthlessly. That he was the most feared man in China I could well believe.

"The general says," Ling translated, "that he is happy to see you in China. The general wishes to apologize for your quarters. He is flying a foreign chef for you from Hong Kong. He says he will also have an eye specialist flown in. He is much concerned about your health."

Not to be outdone, I replied, "Tell the general I am happy to be in China and to work under his distinguished direction. I am regaining the sight of my eye, and my quarters and food are all that can be desired. Tell him that food means nothing to me and that my only wish is to be of service to China."

The Hatchet Man smiled faintly at this and spoke.

"The general says," Ling translated, "that you are the only adviser he knows who does not complain."

"I have nothing to complain about," I returned, "except that the students do not arrive and that I get little material to work on."

"The students and more material will arrive tomorrow," Ling translated.

After we had discussed plans for some time, I took the Hatchet Man to one of the servants' quarters in the garden. This I had converted into a workshop, where I had installed the two chemists and the engineer supplied me by General Tseng to work with the materials flown in from Hong Kong. I explained the incendiary pencils and the demolition bombs, as I had previously to General Tseng. The Hatchet Man gave me an appraising look. That he was pleased I could see.

"Tell the general," I said to Ling, "that because these men are inexperienced, I removed them as far as possible from my window."

The Hatchet Man nodded approval.

"The general says this work is most important and that you will please keep General Tseng informed. He will himself come again soon to observe progress. He also would like to have you for dinner tonight if you will come. In a few days he will take you to see the Generalissimo."

2

At seven we joined the Hatchet Man in the heatless reception room of the apartment in which I had spent my first night in Chungking. I was glad there were no other guests, for conversation with a number of Chinese through an interpreter is most trying. There was small talk before dinner. The Hatchet Man had admired my stove and had asked Ling to have one made for him. I drew a picture of a larger one, which I was sure could be made by the same craftsman. This pleased the Hatchet Man immensely.

In the damp, unheated room I was slowly perishing for lack of a drink. Then dinner was served, and the general made amends for his seeming neglect by opening a bottle of Five Star

Hennessy, from which he filled three small bowls. He lifted his, drank, and, showing me the empty cup, said, *"Kam-pei."*

Ling and I followed suit. This, I thought, will be quite a party if we *kam-pei* with brandy through twenty courses. I had found it difficult enough to keep fairly sober on yellow wine at a Chinese formal dinner.

I had lost track of the toasts and the number of strange dishes when the Hatchet Man turned on me a fishy eye and demanded, "How did you know Wang Ching-wei was preparing to escape?"

The question was not wholly unexpected, because Number Two had been asking the same thing for the past couple of weeks. Unable to think up a plausible answer, I had ignored him. Clearly, I could not ignore Number One.

The difficulty arose from a visit I had paid Fidelity after a fourth escape from Ling and my guards. She was in her apartment, packing.

"You're not leaving us?" I said.

"Yes, I am leaving." She seemed much disturbed.

"And without a word to me?"

"It was all very sudden. I wasn't sure where I could find you. But I would have left a message with George."

"Of course you're coming back," I said to reassure myself.

"No," she replied. "Not ever."

So, I reflected, Wang Ching-wei, leader of the peace party and enemy of the Generalissimo, was deserting to the Japanese. Japan, which had already set up puppets in Manchukuo and Peiping, was looking for an influential Chinese leader to head the puppet government at Nanking. It all fitted patly. Wang had fallen for their blandishments. He must have powerful forces behind him to dare such a bold and dangerous move. If permitted to escape to the Japanese, he could very well destroy China.

Fidelity came and sat beside me, nervously snapping her heavy purse. A packet of American bank notes fell to the floor.

"You'll never get through the customs with all that," I

warned her, having in mind others who had been stripped and searched. China was conserving foreign exchange.

"That's the least of my worries," she said a bit impatiently. "They would not dare touch me."

She handed me a card in her writing. "That's my name in Chinese. You understand the address?"

"Yes, of course."

"You won't like it here," she said confidently. "You will be going back to the States soon. If you pass through Hanoi, send me a chit by messenger."

She rose. "You must go now. They will be here for me any time." She gave me her hand and smiled. "Be careful," she said, suddenly serious. "And" — she paused — "don't trust George."

Wang has told her who I am, I reflected. He has many followers close to the Generalissimo.

Leaving her, I had rushed home and ordered Ling to send the car for Number Two. "It's urgent," I told him.

But Number Two, the fat fool, had only looked at me stupidly when I told him Wang Ching-wei was deserting, escaping by plane to Hanoi around midnight.

"The general says," Ling translated, "that is impossible. He says Wang has no reason to leave."

To this I made no answer.

Ling translated again: "The general asks what makes you think Wang is leaving China?"

"Tell the donkey," I answered disgustedly, "I didn't say Wang is leaving. I said he is deserting. You can say to the general that a little bird told me."

With that I had gone to bed. Number Two had done nothing, and Wang had flown to Hanoi. It wasn't going to be easy to explain all this plausibly to the Hatchet Man. Wang Ching-wei, the deserter, had been read out of the Kuomintang by the Generalissimo, and over two hundred of his followers had been arrested — how many beheaded, I could not learn. Now all the world knew that Wang Ching-wei was to be Japan's puppet in Nanking.

When the Hatchet Man put his question to me, I did not answer at once. He spoke again, and Ling translated: "The general says you eluded your guards four times."

"Yes," I admitted. "I'm not fond of guards."

"Perhaps you saw officials at the American embassy and they told you?" the Hatchet Man said suspiciously.

"No."

"Then how did you know?"

His voice was no longer polite, and I knew it was up to me to concoct a plausible story.

"There is really no mystery about it, General," I said. "I was at a teahouse, alone. Chinese walls between dining rooms are thin. I overheard a conversation in German."

"You know who spoke?"

"No. I did not see them. There are many Germans here. You have German advisers — why, I do not know, because they are Japanese sympathizers. Does not Wang Ching-wei himself speak German?"

The Hatchet Man clearly wasn't satisfied with my explanation. But the fact remained that I had given warning and that it was due to no fault of mine that Wang had escaped. His voice regained its warmth.

"The general says Number Two was stupid not to listen to you. He says also that he is responsible for your safety and that it is dangerous for you to be alone."

"Tell him I like my freedom but that I promise to be more careful in future."

We drank two more bowls of raw brandy with the usual *kam-pei.* My head reeled, and the general, like all Chinese after a few drinks, was red to his party-uniform collar.

"Ask the general to tell me about the assassination in Tientsin of Miss Yoskimiko Kamashma. In America she is thought a romantic person. The story goes that she is the daughter of a Manchu prince and his Japanese concubine, that she seduced Henry Pu-yi to become the puppet emperor of Manchukuo, and that she betrayed her first husband to the Japanese. How was she killed?"

"The general says she died yesterday. But yesterday he was in Chungking, so he couldn't know much about it."

The Hatchet Man smiled faintly, and I grinned back.

"Tell the general I think Wang Ching-wei should be killed before he does China too much harm."

"The general says you are the first foreigner he has met who believes that personal enemies of his country should be liquidated."

"Why not?" I returned. "In war an assassin's bullet is no more than a soldier's, to my way of thinking, and quite as patriotic. Western tradition says differently. There is an unwritten law that the leaders should go unharmed while the pawns slit each other's throats. Napoleon bled Europe for years without suffering a scratch. One assassin's bullet would have saved countless lives and untold suffering. In the American Civil War the Confederate general Robert E. Lee, by his military genius, dragged out the war for four long years. Assassination is not pleasant, but neither is war."

This called for another *kam-pei*. Ling had quit long ago, the general blinked and gulped his brandy, and I must have been far gone myself. I heard myself say, as from a distance, "Ask the general if his men use silencers."

"Silencers? What is that?" Ling asked.

"Well, it's like this," I began gropingly. "I come from a family of poachers in southern Indiana. We know how to make a contraption that we screw on the end of a rifle barrel. So when we sneak into the woods where there are 'No Hunting' signs to kill a few squirrels, the gun makes no noise. In America some of our gangsters attach silencers to their revolvers. Tell the general that if his men are after Wang Ching-wei, they should use silencers."

The subject being obscure to Ling, it took him some time to

explain. Finally he said, "The general asks if you can make one."

"Tell him yes. With the tools and materials General Tseng brought in from Hong Kong, I can do a first-rate job."

"The general asks how long it will take."

"Ask him how soon he needs it."

"The general says," Ling translated, "he leaves" — he caught himself and continued — "he wants to know if you can make it in two days."

"Yes," I said, "if he has the right type of gun." I pulled mine out and laid it on the table. "This is the size I want, but mine is an automatic and silencers are not very successful on automatics. I want a revolver, in which the chambers revolve when you pull the trigger."

The Hatchet Man examined the gun while Ling explained.

"The general asks how much noise the silencer makes."

I extracted the clip of shells and the one in the barrel and snapped the trigger. "Not much more than that."

The Hatchet Man smiled widely for the first time. Knowing the custom, I drank but one more *kam-pei* and then rose. The general followed me to my car, shook hands when I got in, and bowed as we drew away.

The chill air revived Ling, who had been the worse for wear. He looked at me owlishly.

"Old saying among Chinese that he who plays with tiger had better watch his pants."

"The Hatchet Man and I," I replied, "are like that." I held up two fingers close together.

Ling when tight does not always show me the respect due a distinguished foreign adviser. He made a vulgar sound.

"The hell you say," I replied.

Indeed, as I sobered I felt it might be well not to push the new intimacy too far, not to presume on it. My standing with the Hatchet Man depended precisely upon my value to him, the use to which he could put me.

• *Chungking, January 1939*

TONIGHT I ATE ALONE — Chinese pheasant cooked by my newly imported "foreign chef," who is a Chinese. Having a chef lifts me to the level with the Hatchet Man, who takes his with him on his trips. I wonder whether he does so on short excursions for a little quiet assassination. But probably he doesn't do that in person. A boss gangster has gunmen for such purposes.

Ling is somewhere looking for one of the Chinese CNAC co-pilots to ask him to bring me a bottle of cold shots on his next trip to Hong Kong. I also ordered a hypodermic needle, but Ling says their importation is forbidden because of the drug addicts. The Chinese are trying to stamp out the use of opium. To forbid the importation of hypodermic needles seems rather a futile gesture, however, since the Chinese prefer opium pipes. I could have asked the Hatchet Man to get me one, had I known in time. But after trying out the silencer I made for him, he disappeared. Gone to Hanoi, perhaps, on the hunt for Wang Ching-wei. I wish him luck, but I hope Fidelity keeps out of the way. I can't warn her without tipping off the boss's hand.

Houseboy Lao Tsai, after serving me dinner, began to play the half-dozen cracked records on the gramophone Ling bought me. He's played some sentimental thing by Bing Crosby three times. It fairly drips molasses. I asked, "You like music?" and he answered, "Music goodee."

I haven't yet learned why the Chinese add the *ee* sound to English words. I must ask Shon Ging to tell me. When I ask Ling, I get a wisecrack for answer.

The ancient Buddhist temple next to me, though mostly in ruins, shelters about a hundred war orphans. It is unheated, but the children in their padded gowns seem not to mind. They sing and drill a great deal when it's not raining and apparently are quite happy. I bought forty chickens for their Christmas dinner — though I doubt if they know anything about Christmas — and the old toothless Buddhist monk who looks after them paid me a polite call and bowed his thanks. I hope to learn something of their religion, but Ling, who scoffs equally at Buddhists and Christians, hasn't helped me much so far. He says the Christian missionaries who come up the Yangtze carry a Bible in one hand and a bowl of rice in the other. The Chinese, who cannot understand the Christian idea of immortality, accept the rice but never really become Christians.

"You studied English under a priest," I said. "You told me you were a Christian."

"No," he said. "I did not tell you I was a Christian. I told the priest I was a Christian. English lessons for Buddhists, five dollars. For Christians, one dollar."

"The propaganda minister," I persevered, "tells us the Generalissimo is a Christian and reads the Bible every day."

"The propaganda minister also gives out" — and Ling smiled sardonically — "that America loan China fifty million gold dollars."

"Ling," I said severely, "I didn't know hypocrisy was a Chinese characteristic."

Ling shrugged.

"Ancient ancestor say" — he grinned — " 'Crows are black everywhere.' "

2

On Christmas Eve I gave a dinner, "foreign style," at a White Russian restaurant for Ling's little friend, who was leaving the next day for Kweiyang to study music. Lu Shon Ging, whom I hadn't seen since the Hatchet Man closed my chateau to visitors, was also there, as demure as ever. For the first time the girls drank imported French wine, a gift to me from the Hatchet Man. This time when I escorted Shon Ging home she wasn't embarrassed by foul-mouthed coolies, for she was well escorted — the chauffeur and two guards in the front seat of the car and the four of us in the back. Then I dropped Ling and his friend downtown and was driven back to my prison.

I was still working on some documents when Ling returned at 3:00 A.M. I got out a bottle and helped him drown his sorrow over the departure of his sweetheart. He can't marry her, because he already has a wife and three children, not to mention a mother-in-law and an old father, on their way upriver from Hankow.

"Why don't you make her your concubine?" I asked.

He shook his head mournfully.

"Why not? Isn't it a Chinese custom?"

"Sometimes, yes, but I am too poor," he said.

"Then you're in a hell of a fix," I said cheerfully.

He managed a sickly grin. "That is true, Adviser."

I poured us another drink of the Hatchet Man's best whiskey.

"There are some," I remarked, "who say that intimacy is the cure for love sickness."

Ling nodded gloomily. "Ancient saying, 'To sleep with woman make solitary couch pleasant.'"

"There's your answer," I suggested.

"No, Adviser," Ling answered. "You not understand Chinese custom. She could not marry. In Chinese marriage boy place silk handkerchief beneath girl on wedding night. If she is virgin he give handkerchief to his mother, who sends it to bride's parents with a roast pig. If bride not virgin she go back to parents. No roast pig and no marriage."

"Drink your whiskey," I said. "Sometime you will be a rich merchant with many concubines."

This was two weeks ago. Today he received a letter from his beloved, saying she wants to take up medicine instead of marriage as a career and offering herself to him. Now he is all on fire and urges that we visit the front by way of Kweiyang.

· Chungking, January 1939

THIS AFTERNOON I WAS TAKEN to the Generalissimo by General Tseng, in the absence of the Hatchet Man. The appointment was made yesterday, and Ling, who always wears foreign clothes, was ordered to appear in party uniform. The Generalissimo disapproves of Western styles for his men. Ling rushed to a tailor and was to have his uniform by 2:00 P.M. today. At noon he got the coat and at two the pants. The uniform, even to the brass buttons, is the same as that worn by American officers during the World War, except that the pants are long and the color black or blue-black.

The appointment was for four, and at three I dolled up in a blue suit, purchased in Hong Kong, and my one remaining white shirt with starched collar, saved for this occasion. Chungking natives, unlike the Cantonese laundrymen in the States, haven't learned to starch and iron collars and cuffs.

General Tseng showed up shortly before four, and we followed his car in mine. Most of the headquarters buildings are downtown, but Tseng's car headed for the suburbs. At the edge of the city we turned up a hill and stopped before a two-story gray brick house behind a high brick wall. A few cars were parked in an open space in front. The general handed an envelope to one of the four sentries, who, after reading it, ushered us through the gate, up a few steps, and into a large front yard. Along the wall were lookouts with armed sentries.

The house itself, of perhaps ten rooms, was unpretentious.

(Without a word being spoken, a Chinese in a blue gown took our hats and coats, and we were led into a small room furnished with a bare table and four straight-backed chairs.) There was an open fireplace — the first I've seen here — burning charcoal, and the floor was covered with small cheap native rugs. The walls were painted white and the windows draped with cheap blackout cloth. There were no flowers, pictures, or scrolls.

One of the Generalissimo's many secretaries, a young Chinese named Li, also in native dress, introduced himself in English. Through an open double door I could see perhaps ten other native-dressed Chinese talking in low tones. We, too, talked in whispers — just why, I don't know. Ling, with the difficult job of translating to do, was nervously wiping the perspiration from his hands. The tension, which I too shared, was broken by the entrance of a huge creature in a brilliant blue uniform covered with decorations — the French military attaché, no doubt. At this entrance, Mr. Li took us into another room, where we were served tea and the inevitable hot towels. I did my best to carry on a conversation, but Ling and General Tseng remained nervously silent.

Finally, still another Chinese opened the door, bowed, and Ling and the general motioned me to precede them. We followed the Chinese down the hall a few steps and into a large room simply furnished. Here, too, the walls were bare and the windows draped with blackout curtains. At the far end, in front of a cushioned chair beside an open fireplace, stood a thin man in yellow khaki and black-cloth Chinese slippers. He wore no military belt, decorations, or insignia of any kind.

I paused in the doorway, awaiting some signal from him. He bowed his head slightly and motioned with his right hand, indicating a couch. There was no word spoken, no introduction. I stood momentarily to his right. He motioned for me to be seated, then to Ling and the general. We sat down, and I saw we had been followed by Mr. Li and a Chinese shorthand writer, who quickly seated himself and bent over his pad. This surprised me, for I had not known Chinese could be recorded in shorthand.

I was seated within three feet of the Generalissimo and so was able to observe him closely. His hair was closely cropped at the sides and was perhaps no longer than a half-inch on top of his head. His graying mustache was closely cut. I felt I was in the presence of a scholar or sage rather than of a great leader.

He looked directly into my eyes and spoke. Ling translated, "The Generalissimo asks if this is your first visit to China?"

I told him yes, but that I had read a great deal about China. After this was translated he looked at me again and spoke.

Ling translated, "The Generalissimo says he has heard about you for many years."

I thought to myself, He's read the Chinese version of my book, *The American Black Chamber,* for which I had received not a penny in Chinese royalties. However, this seemed not the time or the place to mention that, so I said to Ling, "Even the schoolchildren in America know about the Generalissimo and Madame Chiang Kai-shek." As Ling translated, a pleased smile spread over the Generalissimo's face.

Evidently a definite routine of polite palaver introduces the conversations of Chinese officials with foreigners, for this followed a pattern to which I was accustomed. However, when, in answer to his polite questions about my welfare, I stated that I hungered for English conversation, he seemed sincere in requesting Mr. Li to send me English-speaking Chinese who could be trusted. I think he also meant it when he said, "If at any time you are not comfortable, you must come and tell me."

He then asked me about my work and listened attentively while I answered, interrupting me now and then with a shrewd question. At last he glanced at a sheet of paper on a small table at his right — other appointments, I guessed — rose, gave my hand a firm grasp, bowed, and smiled faintly. At the door I paused and, emulating my Chinese companions, bowed. He was still standing, a thin and rather lonesome man, or so he seemed to me.

The servants helped us into our coats, the sentries at the gate saluted, and as we drove away a small squad of soldiers arrived — a change of guard, I imagined.

· *Chungking, February 1939*

THIRTY STUDENTS, some of whom were educated in Japan and speak and read Japanese, have arrived and settled into the hard routine of analyzing Japanese intercepts brought with them from Hankow. Most of these look more or less like the following:

With the students came another interpreter, named Wu Fou. Born in Hawaii, he speaks fluent if ungrammatical English; educated in Germany as an engineer, he speaks pidgin German.

My students were gathered together a year ago but have not the faintest idea how to begin the attack on our material. I doubt they will ever know. I give them a prepared lecture each day, but what they understand of it is questionable. I doubt that the interpreters themselves understand, and even if they do, they still have the problem of making themselves clear to thirty people who speak eight different dialects. Fortunately, both Ling and Wu speak many dialects, or so they say. But from the expressions on the faces of my students, I sometimes wonder.

The Chinese word *shih* with a different inflection means variously *yes, four,* or *ten.* I wagered Wu and Ling that neither could guess what the other had in mind if he would turn his back, write the intended meaning for me on a piece of paper, and pronounce the word. Each guessed correctly less than half the time, much to the students' delight. And the tense in Chinese verbs is absolutely hopeless. I asked Ling to cable the Chinese authorities in Washington, asking whether my monthly salary had been deposited there since my departure. Ling couldn't tell from the answer whether the money *had been* or *would be* deposited. I raised so much hell about it that the finance officer issued me a sight draft in gold, despite the fact that my contract had been lost in the retreat from Hankow and there is no record of my employment. The mere threat that I will wireless the Hatchet Man brings results.

To a man, the students hate Number Two. He has stacked them in bunks in the servants' quarters without heat and with few blankets, like so many cattle. Their work schedule is severe: in the morning, eight to noon, and in the afternoon and at night, two to six and seven to ten. They seldom have time even to do their washing. When they can, they spread their garments all over the garden. How they find sun to dry them is again a miracle, in all this season of rain and heavy mists. Looking out of a morning I see the sodden blue gowns like limp blotting paper draped over stone benches and tea tables.

The students are forbidden to leave the premises without a

pass and have no amusements. So I had a native carpenter make a Ping-Pong table and I imported paddles and balls. When it was set up, Number Two summoned me to his office, which he has installed on the first floor.

"What is the Ping-Pong table for?" he demanded.

"For the students," I replied.

My new interpreter, Wu, translating, dripped vinegar. "The general says that if your students have any extra time, they should use it to better advantage by studying. The fat bastard, may his ancestors suffer from the itch."

Wu's ad-libbing in his translations is going to get one or the other of us into trouble someday.

Number Two listens to my lectures each day, pretending to comprehend and looking wise. Twice a week he calls the students together and harangues them.

"What does he talk about?" I asked Wu.

"Nothing," said Wu. "Just *walla-walla.*"

"What's that?"

"Talkee-talkee, hot air, baloney."

"But what about?"

"Oh, they should work hard, save money, not go to the restaurants or movies, and not be seen with any girls except those approved by the Service."

Moral and edifying discourse is evidently as unpalatable in Chinese as in other tongues.

"How much does the Service pay them," I asked Wu, "that they should save money?"

"Thirty Chinese dollars a month, of which they pay five for food."

The rate of exchange as of today is $7.00 Chinese to $1.00 gold or American.

"I see Number Two at the movies and eating in restaurants," I remarked.

"The damned Donkey," said Wu.

"The Donkey?"

"That's what we call him," said Wu.

I had secretly so named him myself, but Wu's disrespect rather surprised me.

"I see Number Two running around with different women," I persisted. "Why can't the boys do the same?"

"Chinese New Life Movement," said Wu.

"And what," I asked, "is that, in God's name?"

"Chinese rules for living — for everyone but the generals. Girls for generals, concubines for generals, squeeze for generals, but not for government clerks and coolie soldiers."

The Ancient Wisdom of all peoples has a word for it.

• *Chungking, February 1939*

*T*HE CONTINENTAL MORSE TELEGRAPH CODE of dots and dashes for the twenty-six letters of the alphabet and the ten numbers, together with the other signals for comma, paragraph, period, interrogation mark, and the like, is universally the same and is understood by all operators throughout the world. An Oriental operator not only must understand all these signals, but he also must understand the signals for the forty-eight Japanese letters, as well as the many procedure signals. To illustrate the vast number of sounds an Oriental operator must master, I quote the dots and dashes for the Roman alphabet, Arabic numerals, and Japanese letters, which are commonly called *kana:*

Y ケ -..--	E ヘ -.	I い ..
コ ----	D ホ -...	" ..--..
サ -.-..	X マ -..-	/ .----
ン --.-.	⚫ ..-.-	2 ..---
ス -----	T ム -	3 ...--
セ .---.	メ .-..-	4 ....-
ソ ---.	モ -...-.	5 .....
N ヌ -..	W ヱ .--	6 -....
F チ ..-.	ユ -..--	7 --...
P ユ .---.	M ヨ --	8 ---..
テ .-..--	S ラ ...	9 ----.
ト ..-..	G リ --.,	0 -----

Added to this, of course, are punctuation marks, short signals for numerals, and standard procedure signals. What surprises me about the Chinese is their mental alertness in mastering telegraphy, despite their mechanical stupidity and their philosophy of *mien tien* (tomorrow), for they truly believe they should not do today what can well be done tomorrow. A foreign operator is too lazy mentally to learn to write Japanese *kana,* much less master the signals. Instead, he writes down two Roman letters that together have the same signals as one *kana.* For example, if he hears .—.. he will write the letter *a* for .— and *d* for —.. or *ad,* instead of writing the *kana* for which these signals stand.

In World War I, I was chief of Military Intelligence Eight and in charge of intelligence communications and intercepts. I tried to teach our operators to write *kana* and to intercept them as such, but without the faintest success. Everywhere I find Americans loath to learn a language — it's so much easier to speak English and force the other fellow to do the same.

Here I certainly have a problem, for there are no Japanese typewriters anywhere, and *kana* statistics of messages must be recorded by hand. However, at least I have uniform reception and recordings.

I have been studying a series of intercepts that we hear every day at 6:00 A.M., noon, and 6:00 P.M. Their similarity stands out if they are recorded one beneath the other:

May No 1 ソフナ フラヌ ヨイウ キラム ラフヨ

" " 2 ソフナ フラヌ ヨイウ キイソ ラナソ

" " 3 ソフナ フラヌ ヨイウ キラヌ ラヌソ

" " 1 ヌフラ ラヨフ ナフラ ウライ

" " 2 ヌヌナ ラヨキ ナヌキ ウヨラ

" " 3 ヌラソ ラヨフ ナフソ ウライ

It was while recording some of these messages that I discovered only ten *kana* were being used, whereas there are forty-eight *kana* in the Japanese alphabet. Why is this? I asked myself. Why only ten *kana*? These must represent figures, I thought. The Japanese, to speed up transmission, are using ten *kana* with short signals to represent the ten numerals. After some study I made up the following table to convert the *kana* to numerals, which enabled me to work much faster, since statistical charts could be recorded on a typewriter:

1 2 3 4 5 6 7 8 9 0

ヌ フ ラ ヨ イ ム ナ キ ウ ソ

Also, to the uninitiated, repeated sequences are more easily seen and remembered.

Using this conversion table, I converted all the intercepts into figures. Eight of the messages are quoted:

```
Msg No 1 Sent 6 A.M. 027 231 459 836 324 123 342 723 935
   "    2   "      "   027 231 459 850 370 117 348 718 943
   "    3   "      "   027 231 459 831 310 130 342 720 935
   "    4   "   noon   027 248 459 870 324 117 326 720 950
   "    5   "      "   027 248 459 876 362 124 390 713 970
   "    6   "      "   027 248 401 880 324 151 315 718 950
   "    7   " 6 P.M.   027 267 459 836 360 130 318 730 931
   "    8   "      "   027 267 459 831 324 125 320 715 940
```

All eight of the messages begin with the group 027, which probably identifies them as coming from Chungking. The first three messages were sent at 6:00 A.M. on different days, and the second group of each is 231. This probably equals "6 A.M." Messages 4, 5, and 6 were sent at noon. The second group in each is 248, which may represent "noon." Similarly, 267 in Messages 7 and 8, sent at 6:00 P.M., may equal "6 P.M."

All the messages are of the same length, and beginning with the third group, the first figure of all the code words is the same in all of the eight messages. Experience tells me these are meteorological messages, giving the weather, ceiling, visibility, barometer readings, temperature, dew point, and wind direction and velocity.

The third group in all the messages is 459, except in Message No. 6, where it is changed to 401. We have had a light rain for several days, so 459 may mean just that, I thought. Also at noon, when Message No. 6 was sent, the skies had cleared. Could 401 equal "weather fair"? I asked myself.

It was just 1:00 P.M. when this occurred to me.

"Wu," I said, "call in the Donkey."

"General," I said after he had settled his fat body in my best chair, "I have a message here that makes me believe Chungking will be bombed this afternoon." I hadn't told him I suspected these intercepts were meteorological messages nor that I myself had made superficial directional tests indicating that the sender was somewhere close to Chungking.

Wu repeated my analysis to the Donkey; then I went over it

all again with Ling, who also translated, but I made no impression. Not sure that my interpreters themselves understood, I sent for a youngster named Chu, who seemed to take a liking to ciphers and who, I believed, understood part of my lectures.

Then, with both Wu and Ling translating, I repeated my whole analysis. Chu now began to point out repetitions in the messages with excited exclamations.

"What's he say?" I asked.

"Chu says the Adviser is right."

But the Donkey still could not understand and asked Chu to go through the analysis step by step. Then suddenly from below the cliff along the river came the terrifying wail of sirens. This was no warning. It was the emergency. In an alert the sirens strike an even, monotonous pitch, but now the sirens rose and fell like the shriek of a banshee. I had heard many warnings in Chungking but never the emergency, for hitherto the Japanese bombers had avoided the fogs and passed north of us to Chengtu, where the weather was usually clear.

There was a mad scramble for the Monks' Cave, led by the Donkey, priceless documents forgotten in the excitement. Wu and Ling looked expectantly at me.

"Go ahead," I said. "I'm afraid of that cave. If they come directly over, I'll get under the stone arch at the well." But though they turned sallow at the sound of approaching bombers, they refused to budge. I noted too that the coolie cooks, guards, laborers, and houseboys also remained to watch.

From my veranda we could see them as they cut across the tip of the city. Nearly all the bombs dropped harmlessly in the Little River, but we learned later a few hit a cheap teahouse and killed some two hundred of Chungking's poor.

I had made a wild guess, and now my reputation was made. But how to locate and capture the sender? This would not be simple, especially with the small amount of wireless equipment available.

· *Chungking, February 1939*

I HAVE NOW REGAINED half the sight of my right eye, and the doctor assures me it will continue gradually to improve. Also, I have finally shaken off my terrible cold. Considering the handicaps I am under, I have had reasonable success in my work, too. Nevertheless, I am more depressed than at any time since my arrival.

Primitive China gets me down. It is too much for me. Perhaps the lack of female companionship contributes to my mood, for Fidelity has gone to Hanoi, and Lu Shon Ging is now in college at Chengtu. I am fond of my students, but sometimes I simply cannot endure their incessant coughing and spitting into the spittoons around the desks. Though I am not a squeamish person, it seems sometimes as though I can't bear the sight of another spittoon. When I show Chu, one of my pet students, what I have done, he leans over me and makes gurgling sounds, drinking mouthfuls of scalding water.

All, all, without exception, drink soup like toads inhaling flies. I often invite some of them to dinner with me in my sitting room, but I no longer serve soup to my guests.

Ling one day asked, "Why doesn't the cook serve soup anymore?"

"I don't know," I said.

"I know." He grinned. "Why don't you teach the students Western manners?"

"Go to hell," I told him.

If ever I am asked when I return home what I remember best about China, I shall say, "Four hundred and fifty million Chinese rising to greet the dawn, coughing, spitting, and blowing their noses."

2

I subscribed to American magazines at Hong Kong, but none has arrived. The one copy of *Time* that I have seen is five months old. The daily sheet called a newspaper is, of course, in Chinese. Yet I buy it out of habit when I am on the street. The night after the bombing, when I got home with Ling, I pulled one out of my pocket, and Chu, who was in my sitting room, laughed.

"What's so funny?" I asked Ling.

"Chu laughs because you always buy a newspaper and can't read it."

Ling translates for me only when I ask him to. I said, "Well, you can read it. What does it say?"

"It says a few tons of bombs dropped."

"How many dead?" I asked.

"It says a few hundred dead."

"How many wounded?"

"It doesn't say — just a few hundred dead."

Ling and Chu are both very matter of fact about death, but as we watched the pieces of dead coolie men, women, and children being gathered up and borne away, I saw them put handkerchiefs to their eyes to hide the tears.

Yesterday, in search of diversion to dispel my low spirits, I kept a downtown rendezvous with an English-speaking Chinese owner of a small tea shop. He was surprised when I showed up driving my car, alone. My new friend, Yang, served me tea and some vile Chinese white wine that smells and tastes like Kentucky moonshine but that the Chinese rave about and serve at all formal functions. Two giggling Chinese girls in padded blue gowns joined us, and I suggested that we drive to the country-side for luncheon.

The car is a right-hand drive, but I forgot for a moment that in the Orient you drive on the left side of the street. Ling says this is an ancient Chinese custom that enables one to fight better with the sword in the right hand, but I am skeptical, for I have yet to see a Chinese who wants to fight.

I nearly ran down a line of ricksha coolies. Because there are no bridges over the Yangtze and I was afraid to wait for a ferry lest Ling and my guards find me, I took the one road leading to the country. Here, too, Ling and his aides might have attempted to stop me.

"Keep your eye out for my interpreter," I told Yang, and with long blasts of the horn scattered the crowd that had gathered. Without mishap, though with many near accidents, we reached the Chengtu Road, which penetrates rolling hills to the northwest. To drive on the left side of the road is confusing at first, especially when every moment a pedestrian steps in front of you. Either you knock him down or just graze him, and, like a chicken, he may jump in either direction.

"Yang," I asked, "why do these natives keep stepping in front of the car?"

"Oh," he answered in his best English, "Chinaman believe devil after him. Chinaman get in front of car, jump away. But devil he get killed."

"Does it help if foreign devil drives the car?"

"Sure, sure." He laughed and translated for the two girls. The one at my side grinned and nodded. I thought her really pretty.

About ten miles out we found a dingy, evil-smelling teahouse and stopped for luncheon. We ordered a number of dishes, together with hot wine, for it was cold and damp within. While we waited to be served, I asked Yang where I could find a toilet. He said he didn't know and spoke to my companion.

"She says use spittoon."

I didn't enjoy my holiday, but on my return I had some fun

at the expense of Ling and Wu, when they came dashing from the gate of the chateau, followed by the chauffeur. I switched off the ignition and pocketed the key before they got to the car. Then I put on the brakes and stepped out.

Wu, a graduate engineer, began arguing with the chauffeur, who displayed his keys. They tried to start the car without a key. Then Wu inserted the chauffeur's key and the engine responded.

"How'd you start it without a key, Adviser?" Wu asked.

"Ignition wires crossed, I guess," I answered and left them. Over my shoulder I could see Wu lifting the hood to examine the wires. It would take them some time to figure this one out, I thought, though the chauffeur would ultimately tumble to the answer.

In the absence of Ling one afternoon, I had played rather a low trick on the chauffeur. We were alone but for my houseboy.

"Lao Tsai," I said, "ask Lao Fong if he like wash in bathtub."

"He likee." Lao Tsai grinned.

No Chinese employer, supposing, as was improbable, that he *had* a bathtub, would ever permit such a thing. But while the chauffeur luxuriated in the Adviser's tub and composed a tale for his friends, I searched his pockets and made an impression of the ignition key to the car.

Wu and Ling came to my room after looking over the car.

"Did you find the trouble, boys?" I asked.

Wu spat judiciously, after the American fashion.

"You ain't pulling no miracles on me," he said. "Did you get a kick out of breaking away?"

"No," I said sourly, "I didn't."

"That's ten times you have escaped," said Ling. "Old saying, 'Man steal once maybe mistake. Ten times, habit. Cut off head.'"

"Am I a prisoner?" I asked.

Wu grinned. "The Donkey is mad. He wants to see you. He's downstairs."

Herbert O. Yardley in the 1930s, before leaving for China

"Tell him nuts," I said. "Also tell him that my contract expires next Monday and that I'm going home."

3

In just what words my message would have been conveyed to the Donkey I was not to learn, for sounds of excitement in the garden below called me to the veranda. Ling yelled up at me, "Hu Yeh has hanged herself!"

Snatching hat and coat, I rushed downstairs. Lao Fong had started the car. Wu, Ling, and I climbed in. I turned to see the Donkey waddling down the path.

"Hold it," I said. "Here comes Number Two."

"To hell with the Donkey!" Wu cried. "*Tso-la,*" he yelled at Lao Fong, and with horn screaming, we caromed down the narrow muddy road.

Hu Yeh was the youngest of my students and the only girl. Self-effacing and shy, she colored and bowed timidly every time I spoke to her.

"What's this all about?" I asked, because I couldn't conceive of this gentle creature taking her own life. I looked at Wu's dark face. I had suspected that he and Hu Yeh were sweethearts and secretly engaged. Wu sat with averted head and did not answer.

Ling said, "I don't know."

"It's like this, Adviser," Wu said at last. "We have just heard what Lao Fong tells. Yesterday Hu Yeh asked the Donkey's permission to visit her dying mother downriver. The Donkey refused, and Hu Yeh escaped from the grounds, only to be caught at Tai Ping Men, where she was trying to get a downriver boat. They put her in jail. Why didn't she tell me? You would have interceded for her."

"Of course," I said, amazed at how much went on about me of which I knew nothing.

We found her in a criminal's steel cage, surrounded by the dirty scum of Chungking — drug addicts, thieves, prostitutes. One of them had cut the body down. Chinese girls wear, in lieu of elastic, a cord around the waist to tuck their panties under. It was this Hu Yeh had used.

There was nothing I could do. I said to Wu, "I'll leave you the car and walk back."

At two in the morning the Donkey sent a messenger for Wu and Ling. I heard them come back at daylight and called to them. Ling was obstinately silent, but Wu, very bitter, told me what the Donkey had said.

"The damned fool thinks you avoid your guards to communicate with the enemy."

"That's a pleasant thought," I said.

"He wants to set a trap for you."

"You mean he wants to frame me."

"No, a trap."

"You can't trap a man into doing what he doesn't do. It looks like a frame-up to me."

"He don't know nothing," Wu said. "He's just suspicious. He's stupid, but he's dangerous, too. You'd better stick with your guards."

"So," I said. "Well, we'll have a long talk with the Donkey after breakfast. Get to bed." They hesitated to leave. "Go ahead. Don't worry. I won't say a word about tonight."

When the Donkey came puffing into my office about noon, he must have known we were in for a battle, for I didn't rise as usual. He stood awkwardly until I pointed to the chair before my desk, into which he subsided.

"Tell him," I said to Ling, "that my contract expires Monday and that I have decided to return to the States. When you answer, cut out the goddamned palaver. And don't preface what I have to say with palaver, either." Turning to Wu, I said, "That goes for you, too."

"Okay," Wu said and contrived to smirk.

The three went into a long exchange of remarks unintelligible to me.

"What goes on here?" I demanded after a time.

Wu shrugged. "The usual crap."

"What else?"

"He says the contract gives China an option on your services for one year, beginning Monday. Also, you are a colonel in the Chinese army and therefore subject to military orders."

Trickery. But nevertheless I was frightened.

"Tell him I don't know what was in the contract written in Chinese. That, I didn't sign. I signed an English translation made by the Chinese authorities in Washington. Also," I lied, "a photostat of that contract is on file with my government. I am not a colonel in the Chinese army and took no oath. I was damned careful not to lose my citizenship. China has no option on my services. Tell him I'll have no monkey business. If he doesn't release me voluntarily, I'll go to the airfield Tuesday accompanied by the American military attaché and American newspapermen to see that my departure is not prevented."

I had laid it on pretty thick, but it seemed the thing to do. While the three thrashed all this out, I poured each a drink of brandy from the bottle in my desk.

"*Kam-pei,*" I said.

"*Kam-pei,*" said the Donkey, choking on the words.

"Now what?" I asked.

"He thinks you are playing an American trick and just want more money." Wu's smile was derisive.

"Tell him he's already paying me too much."

Wu shrugged. "He'll understand even less than he does now. But keep after him. You have him down."

The best defense is to attack, I remembered. "Ask him this: Why does he tell me he has a hundred operators intercepting messages? I know for a fact he has only seven. I've compared the handwriting of the operators on all messages. There are seven men and no more."

I had previously discussed this with Wu, who had told me the Donkey was trying to save face. China had lost two hundred operators in Hankow when the Donkey had run away without arranging for their escape. Now they were either dead or prisoners of Japan.

"He says you misunderstand. He says he is training one hundred operators, not that he has them."

"Ask him why he let Hu Yeh hang herself?"

Wu's face was dark and his voice harsh.

"He says it was for discipline and crap of that sort."

The man is a fool and a coward and a liar, I thought. I had known it before, and this incident proved it.

"Get a pencil," I said to Wu, "and take this down, word for word. I will sign another six months' contract, English not Chinese, at my present salary, but only on these terms. First, the students' hours on weekdays will be from eight A.M. to six-thirty P.M., with two hours off for lunch and a siesta. On Sundays, the hours will be from eight A.M. to one P.M. After work, the students may leave the grounds, returning by one A.M. Passes will be required by those remaining out all night or for any extended leave. I am to be consulted before passes are refused. Salaries are to be increased to one hundred dollars, and nothing is to be deducted for food. The Service budget for food per person is to be increased by twenty percent.

"Second, I am to be free to visit the wireless training school once a week to observe the students' progress and to supervise training methods.

"Third, I am to be given personal freedom. I shall be the sole judge of where I shall live and the friends I entertain. Guards will accompany me on my request."

While they talked over my ultimatum, I walked out to the veranda, fearful that I'd demanded too much and would have to back down. I really wanted to do something for China. Wu had warned me that I'd have to beat the Donkey's ears back to get along with him. "He's a stubborn stupid ass," Wu had said.

But it's easy to beat a donkey so hard that he merely becomes more stubborn and balky than before.

My interpreters finally called me in.

"He says he can grant you permission to visit the wireless students, but he can do nothing more without the consent of Number One."

"Then wireless Number One. I'll wait ten days for an answer."

"He wants to know where you wish to live."

"Anywhere, just so I have freedom and privacy."

"He thinks perhaps you are looking for a girl." Wu smiled.

"Aren't we all?"

"He says few girls fit for the Adviser. He says there is a girl in our Service at Chengtu who can be trusted. He says he will telegraph her to come to Chungking. She will be the Adviser's concubine." Ling and Wu winked slyly in unison.

"If you're not pulling my leg," I said, laughing, "you can tell him to go to hell."

I filled the glasses again and lifted mine to the Donkey.

"*Kam-pei,*" I said.

"*Kam-pei,*" he answered with a smile.

But it wasn't a friendly smile.

· Chungking, March 1939

NUMBER ONE IS STILL AWAY, but the Donkey must have heard from him, because he offered me a new contract for one year and agreed orally to my demands for my students and also for my own freedom. I signed the contract in English, so that there would be no weasel clauses, and reduced the term to six months. As a peace offering, and doubtless at the command of the Hatchet Man, a Hong Kong daily newspaper and American magazines will be flown to Chungking for me.

Ling, Wu, and I made a survey of suitable living quarters. There are a number of three-story walk-up apartments, but few have bathrooms, and the apartments are so close to the city that I feel sure they will be bombed as soon as the spring sun clears the fogs. Finally I found a mud or adobe hut with black-tile roof and pine floors near completion two miles west of the city. It has a Chinese kitchen of earth ranges, a bathroom, servants' quarters, a large reception room, and three bedrooms.

The rent is $165 a month Chinese, or about $16 gold at the present rate of exchange. The hut cost perhaps $3000 Chinese. All real estate, I am told, is rented at a price to repay the cost in two years. Normal interest rates are 20 percent a year, and for speculative ventures the rate is 50 percent. What the effects of such interest rates and rents must be on the Chinese farmers, workers, and small industrialists can be guessed. Four hundred and fifty million Chinese are enslaved to a handful of money-lenders and landowners. Add to these conditions the extortionate taxes and corrupt administrators, and the overall picture is a terrible one. More than the defeat of Japan is necessary to free the Chinese. Abuses that have existed for hundreds and thousands of years will need to be swept away. The monied and landed classes will have to relinquish some of their wealth and power. Vast political and economic reforms are needed. It is difficult for an outsider to see promise of such reforms. China is in the process of change. But it will become what? Not all that the Western world, with its ideals of democracy and equality, has been led to expect.

The interest rate on so speculative a venture as this hut or on brick apartments is 30 percent. The children who carry bricks from the junks at the river bank are paid one penny each. The children, mostly girls, climb five hundred steps from the river, make but two trips a day, and the load of bricks strapped to their backs equals their age. A child of six carries six bricks. Twelve bricks per day earns a wage of twelve pennies, or about one penny gold. Such slave labor is exploited and condemned by those who have inherited the mantle of Sun Yat-sen, the revolutionary.

My Chinese friend Yang complains that he is making only 200 percent profit a year from his stinking teahouse. I fancy he'll make less when the skies are clear and the bombers come. As for myself, I anticipate with these bombings an ever-falling exchange rate, and conduct my own financial affairs accordingly. The rate, which was six to one when I came, is now ten to one. If it continues to fall, it may be twenty to one within a year. So instead of converting gold at ten to one for spending money, I deposit my gold at the Bank of China and borrow Chinese dollars at 20 percent interest. Within a year, $100 in gold may buy $2000 Chinese, whereas I shall pay but $1200 Chinese for my loan of a thousand. If my guess is correct, I shall be $800 Chinese to the good, and the only loser will be the moneylenders. Who are these Chinese Shylocks that I should weep for them?

I had the walls of my new adobe hut painted, but the clay was so damp that the paint was absorbed. So I put a pan of charcoal in each room and left a coolie to watch the fires. The next day when Ling and I drove out to the hut we found the poor devil half-dead from the charcoal fumes. I rushed him to the hospital, where he is rapidly recovering and for the first time in his life eating good food.

Though my hut is away from the city, it is near a cluster of bamboo huts and small rice and vegetable fields. The community outdoor toilet is only twenty yards from my street windows. It is an open vault from which the excrement is salvaged to fertilize the rice and vegetable fields. The stench is indescribable. Ling and I bargained with the community leader, and for $100 Chinese he agreed to transfer the vault farther from my windows. But when the wind blows from it in my direction, the advantage is slight. The Chinese have maintained the fertility of their soil by their fertilizing methods. That is all to the good. We in the West too often impoverish the soil. What China needs is a series of sewage disposal works that salvages what is valuable and converts it into commercial fertilizer — but free from odor and all the disease germs that make raw foods a menace in China. I think I shall apply for the sewage disposal concession after this war is over. I shall become richer than the Rockefellers and have many more concubines.

We searched the town and luckily found enough screening for our needs. I purchased native furniture — a wicker bamboo settee and chairs to match, straight pine dining room chairs, clothes cupboards, native rugs, and the like. Also, I had another stove made like the one that had proved so useful. My bed is a native one with a thin cotton mattress and grass pillows. I tried to get down pillows, but the foreign embassies had thought of it first and cleaned out the city. My prize is a native-made box couch with foreign springs. Over the windows I have draped red and green silk curtains hung from bamboo poles, and Wu surprised me by making lampshades covered with pink silk — he must be colorblind. I am no longer a foreign devil but have now become a foreign prince.

Everything was going along nicely until the Donkey butted in and demanded one of the bedrooms. To keep peace, I let him have it — I was practically forced to, for the Service had insisted on reimbursing me for my outlay, doubtless at the Hatchet Man's prompting. However, I have a reception room and two bedrooms for my own, one of which I have converted to a private sitting room. These two are adjoining and separated by a hall from the rest of the place. Though reduced thus to a two-room apartment, I have a bolt to my door and — I hope — privacy.

Yang, the merchant, was the one who helped me most in furnishing my place. It was he who found the springs for the box couch. To return his kindness I told him he and I would celebrate my first evening as a householder by having dinner together.

I had myself driven downtown to pick him up, and while he waited for a business appointment we sat at a table and had a few cups of hot wine. A few tables away sat two girls in furs. The one facing us smiled and took me in from head to foot — bald head, scarf, white shirt, and shoes. She was very pretty. So, too, the other appeared to be, though her back was to us.

Yang said, "How about taking those two with us to dinner?"

"Do you know them?" I asked.

"Yes, the one who smiled is a distant cousin of mine. And the other is cousin to a friend of mine."

Just then the one with her back to us coughed and blew her nose into the spittoon beside the table. Then she turned to us, her nose still running.

"What do you say, Osborn?" Yang asked.

"Some other time," I said. "There are no spittoons in my place."

· *Chungking, March 1939*

*F*ROM INQUIRIES AT HEADQUARTERS I learn that, although a million Japanese have been killed since the beginning of the war in 1937, but sixty Japanese soldiers are prisoners in Chinese hands. The Generalissimo recognizes the value of prisoners, because there is a standing reward of $20 Chinese for the capture alive of every Japanese soldier. Despite this reward, the coolies prefer to kill their enemies, a fact not to be wondered at, perhaps, since the Japanese are savage little beasts guilty of many atrocities.

I proposed that the sixty captives scattered here and there be brought together in Chungking and questioned for technical information pertaining to my work. My proposal was rejected on the grounds that none was more than a private and would know nothing. Later, word came from Chengtu that a Japanese bomber had crashed, killing all the crew but the bombardier. The Donkey and one of my Japanese-speaking students flew to Chengtu and brought him back. Now he is housed under guard at the chateau. He is a sullen skinny devil but has brightened a little since I insisted that he be well fed and given a bottle of wine now and then. He speaks Mandarin and has been of some value in giving us the full meaning of many Japanese military abbreviations we did not understand.

So far we have learned nothing technical from him, and it may be that he knows nothing. However, I wanted to try scopolamine or sodium amytal on him to make sure. I asked

Wu what he thought, for my experience with Chinese doctors has been such that I hesitated to trust them with the use of the drugs. Wu suggested that we get the Donkey and the Service doctor together to discuss the matter. So a meeting was arranged in the doctor's office.

The doctor is a little fellow, about thirty, smiling and good-humored. He was educated in Germany, but just what that may mean is uncertain. Foreign universities give Chinese students credits whether they have earned them or not, apparently on the theory that they must have learned something and that a little knowledge is better than none — a singularly dangerous theory in the case of doctors, chemists, and engineers.

With Wu interpreting, I explained to the doctor and Number Two the successful use of both sodium amytal and scopolamine in crime detection. I had brought both drugs with me but recommended sodium amytal as the easier to administer. One gram of this dissolved in 20 cc of distilled water is injected into a vein at the rate of 1 cc per minute. As soon as the corneal reflex disappears, which usually requires from 10 to 12 cc of the solution, the injection is stopped. The subject is awakened in about five minutes and questioned. The drug paralyzes the power of reasoning and removes inhibitions, so if the right degree of amnesia is reached, the subject will answer questions truthfully. When, after questioning, he is allowed to sleep for several hours, he will, on awakening, remember only vaguely that he has been questioned, without recalling his replies. The release of inhibitions, I told them, is caused by depression of the cerebrum, which is believed to be the seat of thought and will. There is no center of speech and no center of memory. Consequently, when the power to reason is temporarily suspended, a question going to the cells of hearing is automatically answered. There is no monitor at the switchboard to censor the reply.

The doctor, however inadequate his medical training, understood the theory better than I, and explained further to the Donkey, who continued to look skeptical.

"Will your Japanese prisoner resist injections?" the doctor asked.

"String him up," Wu suggested.

"No," I said. "The prisoner has malaria. We'll tell him the injections are to cure his malaria."

"Excellent," the doctor agreed.

The Donkey thereupon got into a long discussion with Wu and the doctor.

"Number Two is skeptical," Wu told me. "He thinks the whole idea nonsense and is set against it."

There was something back of this, I was sure. Was the Donkey trying to discredit me? I said to Wu, "How about using you as a guinea pig?"

"Not me," said Wu and laughed.

"We'll have to get a volunteer. Any idea?"

"No."

"Well, this is just a stab in the dark. Say to the Donkey that the Adviser has himself taken the drug many times. It is not harmful. Tell him that since he does not believe in the drug, he should prove his disbelief by trying it on himself."

"I'll try it," said Wu, pleased at the prospect.

"Put in a lot of palaver about saving face before the foreigner and all that sort of thing."

Wu must have laid it on, for the uncertainty written on the Donkey's dull features slowly changed to a look of resolution. I almost liked the guy.

"He says okay," Wu translated.

"You must have told him plenty."

"And how!" Wu with difficulty kept a straight face.

I handed the doctor a vial of sodium amytal. The sweat poured from the fat Donkey as the doctor examined his heart and took his blood pressure. But to give the devil his due, he was game, however stupid. Wu and I left the room while the doctor prepared his solution and the Donkey undressed.

When the doctor called us back, the Donkey was lying on a cot, covered with a blanket. The solution, in a graduated glass container, was fed by gravity through a rubber tube attached to a large needle. The doctor with some skill fed 12 cc into a vein in the right arm and then, watching the Donkey's eyes, withdrew the needle. We let him sleep for about five minutes and then directed the doctor to wipe his face with a cold towel. The Donkey, opening his eyes, seemed unsure of his surroundings.

I told Wu to engage him in small talk, whereupon he immediately became talkative. This is the stage at which to test the subject's inhibitions. To prove the action of the drug effective, it was necessary to have him answer some question that normally he would evade or not answer truthfully. I didn't know what to ask, until I remembered questions once asked a young girl under the drug's influence during a test at Northwestern University. Questioned about her sex life, she had readily confessed to two abortions. So I said to Wu, "A pretty Chinese girl had dinner with him at my hut last Tuesday and still another last Friday. Ask him simple questions at first. Ask him, Did you have dinner last Tuesday with a lady friend? Did you have dinner last Friday with a lady friend? Do they live in Chungking? What are their names? See what he says."

Quite an animated conversation ensued.

"You are right," Wu said to me after a bit. "The two girls are married — wives of two of his wireless operators. He says they went to his bedroom."

"Ask him what they talked about."

Amusement succeeded disbelief in Wu's eyes. The doctor chuckled.

"The Donkey says they didn't talk much. They went to bed."

"Both times? On Tuesday and Friday?"

"He says yes."

"Is he going to marry both of them?"

The Donkey laughed when this was put to him.

"He says no," Wu translated and added anxiously, "Is he going to remember what I asked him?"

"No," I reassured him.

"Not even that I called him Donkey?"

"No. Tell the doctor this should prove the efficacy of the drug. Number Two was always very circumspect. Normally he would never have talked as freely as he has."

The doctor expressed himself as fully satisfied, and Wu resumed his questioning of the Donkey. At last he desisted.

"Well?" I said.

Wu was grave. "I asked him a number of questions and he answered them all. He has more power than you realize. It is because he is so feared that he can command these girls. He employs their husbands."

I was afraid we had gone too far. We could not prove to him the power of the drug by recalling such confessions as these. I told Wu to caution the doctor, who proved to be diplomatic.

"The doctor suggests," Wu explained, "that we let the Donkey sleep off the drug. When he wakes, the doctor will tell him only enough to convince him." Wu added regretfully, "Blackmail is out."

Very much out. We could not use our knowledge of the general's derelictions to our advantage. However, it was well to know them. They afforded some protection in possible emergencies. Also, any qualms I had felt in exploiting the Donkey's helplessness were dispelled. He deserved no consideration.

"You must try the drug on the Japanese prisoner tomorrow," I said to the doctor when he bowed and shook hands at the door. He promised to do so and reassured me as to the Donkey's reactions.

"The doctor was quite poetic," Wu told me. "He said, 'Women are made for man's pleasure, and face is not lost in seeking their favors.'"

2

The Donkey was quite affable when he arrived at my office the next morning. He was not self-conscious and evidently bore me

no ill will. The doctor must have played his part well. Wu had
not proved so close-mouthed. The Donkey's confession was too
good to keep, and all the students were snickering behind his
back.

The Donkey ordered that the Japanese prisoner be taken to
the doctor and given the sodium amytal treatment. With us
went a translator of Japanese, Tsu Fu, who convinced the prisoner that the doctor's injections would cure his malaria. But the
experiment proved futile. The prisoner knew nothing of any
value to us. He still has his malaria, and we are without information. However, something has been accomplished. It will be
easy in the future to give others the same treatment, and from
them we may learn something. There are advantages to living
in China. In America the authorities would be afraid to employ
the drug unless the prisoner voluntarily agreed. The same authorities would not hesitate to employ a rubber hose to secure
a so-called confession. I had once suggested to the governor of
New Jersey the use of sodium amytal on Hauptmann, executed
for complicity in the Lindbergh kidnapping case, only to be told
it was illegal. By the method permitted me in China it would
be possible to learn the truth, without resort to brutality or
torture.

When I returned to the chateau after our failure with the
Japanese prisoner, I found General Tseng, chief of sabotage,
drinking hot water in my office. Despite his obesity, he had
climbed the stairs to warm himself at my fire, for the reception
room downstairs was cold and raw. Wu told the general of our
experiments with sodium amytal and gave an expurgated account of the Donkey's confessions, at which the general
laughed.

"He says," Wu told me, "that he would like to try the drug
on his third concubine but that she'd never consent. He says he
has come to see your progress with the explosives and incendiaries."

"Make it very clear," I said, "that it is not *my* progress, but that of *his* chemists and engineer. I've left the whole matter in their hands."

My motive was diplomatic, but I was glad later I had claimed no responsibility.

After we had given the general luncheon, we took him to the shop in the far corner of the grounds where the incendiary devices and bombs were being fabricated. The Donkey and the Japanese interpreter were at that moment returning the Japanese prisoner to his quarters beneath the shop. There he was put to bed, and the door leading to the outside door was bolted.

The Chinese engineer, Chen Huan, kowtowed to his distinguished visitors and led them to his workbench, where all exclaimed over his handiwork: hollow pencils, glass-tube vacuums, and partly completed explosive sticks. I, too, was interested, because I had paid little attention to his progress since giving him drawings and formulae. His two assistant chemists gathered round and put in a word of explanation now and then.

The general and the Donkey were evidently much impressed, but I didn't at all like the way Chen Huan handled the explosives and chemicals. He treated them as casually as lumps of coal. Also, his incendiary and explosive sticks were crudely made and his fingers were all thumbs. I wasn't wholly surprised; I've yet to see a Chinese with mechanical skill.

To demonstrate the white flame that properly compounded incendiaries make, Chen Huan took an iron charcoal pan and placed it on the stone floor. In the bottom he put small quantities of two chemicals an inch or so apart, and picked up a tube of blue liquid.

"What's he doing?" I asked Wu.

"He's going to pour the liquid into the pan to make a flame."

I stepped back. He poured the liquid on the chemicals. Nothing happened. A stupid look came over Chen Huan's face, and all turned and looked questioningly at me. With Wu's help I checked the formula with Chen Huan and discovered that he had left out one chemical. He grinned sheepishly, prepared a second mixture, and repeated the experiment.

"Look out, Wu!" I cried and pulled him back.

A blinding, fierce white flame darted toward Chen Huan, who jumped back from the flame, knocking over as he did so a number of glass tubes and retorts on his workbench filled with chemicals. These instantly burst into white flame, and I yelled to Wu to get everybody out.

We dashed away, and General Tseng, bringing up the rear, fell over a stone tea table. The rest of us ducked behind a stone wall. The explosion that followed rocked the earth and showered us with debris. When I looked out, the shop had all but disappeared.

"The Jap prisoner!" I cried to Wu.

We reached the prison, to find the door blown from its hinges but the prisoner almost unharmed, except for blood in his nose and mouth. My students were all over the place, excitedly asking questions, and a distraught Chen Huan was wildly explaining to General Tseng, who was none the worse but for a dirty uniform and a skinned elbow.

"I think we should have a drink," I said to Wu.

We had scarcely downed the first one when there was a further clamor from below. Wu went to the veranda and returned laughing.

"The prisoner has escaped," he said, "and the Donkey is having fits."

"What's he doing about it?"

"He has ordered everyone out to chase him and has telephoned an alarm to general headquarters."

It was two hours later, and Wu and I were preparing to go downtown for dinner when the Donkey returned.

"They captured the prisoner," Wu said.

"Where?"

"He was sneaking into the British embassy grounds. He thought the British would grant him immunity to capture."

"Well, wouldn't they?"

"They didn't have a chance. The Jap was dragged away before they knew he was there."

"Ask Number Two where they took him."

"They put him in prison. The Donkey says they are going to execute him."

"Execute him!" I exclaimed. "For God's sake, why?"

"The general says the prisoner was most unappreciative. They gave him food and wine and yet he tried to escape."

"But," I said, "you can't execute a man for that."

"The general says why not?"

I digested this. Why not, indeed? I saw I should have to make a different approach.

"Tell the general," I said, "that this Japanese is valuable to us. I want him brought here."

A heated discussion ensued.

"The general says that out of deference to the Adviser he will not execute the prisoner if you can make use of him."

"I want him."

"He says okay."

I found another glass and poured for the three of us.

"*Kam-pei,*" I said.

"*Kam-pei,*" said the Donkey gravely.

It is clear he has done the Adviser a great personal favor in making this concession.

· Chungking, March 1939

THE FOREIGN PRESS reports as follows:

> Wang Ching-wei escaped assassination in Hanoi, French Indo-China, but his secretary and three others were wounded. The gunman fled.

I am wondering if the gunman used my silencer and if Fidelity was mixed up in this.

2

With the approach of spring the fogs that lower over Chungking are thinning and the chill is slowly evaporating from my bones. "Bones" is almost precise, for though I like Chinese food, I have lost thirty pounds since coming here. Except for pork, there is no meat here but water buffalo, and that is too tough to chew. I have imported an ultraviolet ray machine with which to examine documents and discover secret inks. Somewhere I had read that beef subjected to the ultraviolet ray becomes tender. I am a witness to the fact that water buffalo is immune to all such blandishments. I still can't chew water buffalo. Ling can eat it but says even a Chinese stomach tastes it for three days after. He prefers to eat pork three times a day. Since I don't like pork, I subsist largely on poultry.

Already the young plants have broken earth in the rice and vegetable patches near my hut. Yesterday I watched coolies stir the dirt and spray the plants with human fertilizer. Though the stench was terrible, I managed to remain long enough to see how they do the trick. First they take a bucket of excrement from the community pool, add two parts of water, and mix. This they pour into a contraption to which is attached a bamboo blowpipe. Up and down the rows of vegetables they walk, blowing a fine spray of liquid over the plants. Vegetables are already on the market from places nearby that enjoy more sunshine than does Chungking. But after watching the manner of their cultivation, I had Ling buy a large quantity of permanganate of potash, with which the cook is instructed to wash all vegetables before cooking. I trust this will sterilize them. Cholera has broken out and I take such precautions as I can. None of my students has ever had a cholera injection. They don't believe in them. Neither do many Chinese doctors, even those educated abroad.

Despite his aversion to scientific precautions, I made a deal with the Service doctor whereby all my servants and students, my two interpreters, and even the Japanese prisoner were forced to receive cholera, typhoid, and smallpox inoculations. The combined dosage was so great that some of them fainted. But that is a small matter. They may not be interested in preserving their lives, but I am very much interested in preserving mine. The Donkey is away, but when he returns I'll get him, too.

The approach of spring and clearing skies means that the Japanese bombers will soon be over us. We are doing our best, therefore, to find the spy who sends daily meteorological reports by wireless to Hankow, where most of the bombers take off. We continue to intercept his wireless ciphers three times a day — 6:00 A.M., noon, and 6:00 P.M. — and, by comparing the cipher groups to the actual weather — ceiling, visibility, temperature, dew point, wind velocity, and the like — have pretty well reconstructed his code. But we haven't located him, although we are sure he operates from the South Bank.

The Donkey has a makeshift radio plant in South China and has managed to assemble a few sets, including direction finders. Some of his radio students have placed themselves with these at different points on the South Bank, in the hope of discovering the spy's hideout. Several times I have gone with them, taking my own aviation direction finder. It is a small affair, with a dial for tuning in, a loudspeaker that can be cut out and the signals heard through earphones, and a hand much like that on a compass, which is supposed to point toward the sending device. For long-wave signals this works perfectly, but it is inaccurate in locating shortwave transmissions, which for technical reasons most spies employ.

In order not to attract attention, I conceived the idea — not too original — of having Service coolies carry us here and there over the First and Second Ranges of low mountains in sedan chairs, where the sets could be easily concealed. By last Sunday we had restricted the suspect area to the South Hot Springs, a wealthy watering place across the Yangtze where the privileged go for baths and a swim in hot natural springs. I had thought of donning trunks and joining the swimmers, but a few moments' observation of their unhygienic habits in the water put me out of conceit with the notion.

The searchers at 6:00 A.M. had surrounded a shack a few hundred yards up a slope from the town. I was summoned to confirm their readings with my direction finder. I had taken the car, been ferried across the river, and had arrived in good time for the noon reading. An armed guard had been stationed with each operator. If at noon my findings confirmed their readings, the guards were to creep toward the shack and surprise the occupants.

Wu, the Japanese interpreter, a guard, and I — the Donkey was not in evidence — were crowded behind a pine tree near a pagoda and in sight of the shack when, promptly at noon, we caught the signals on 17 kilocycles. My direction finder pointed almost directly at the shack. Wu and I rose and strolled forward as a signal to the others to draw in. Despite my orders not to shoot, my guard fired at a figure that appeared at a window. The signals had stopped without completing the message. Clearly, we had been seen and the spy alerted.

While I was explaining the situation to Wu, the guard suddenly darted from his hiding place and rushed toward the shack, firing as he ran.

"I don't want that Jap killed!" I yelled to Wu and waved him after me.

The Jap was firing from another window and was being fired upon. Fortunately, all were equally poor shots, and no one was hurt. The Jap, cringing and cowed, was captured without a struggle. My car was parked a quarter of a mile away.

"Get the Jap to the car quickly," I told Wu, "while I search the place."

Hurriedly, I searched the hut and found a sending set no larger than a cigar box, together with some dry batteries. In the earth cooking range there were paper ashes — probably his small code. On the person of our prisoner we found a small kit of instruments for gauging the weather — compass, aneroid barometer, Sling psychrometer, and the like. As many of us as possible climbed into the car, and with the others on the running boards, we got away as fast as possible before the natives could learn what was happening.

We took the terrified spy to the Service doctor's, where, at my direction, Tsu Fu, the Japanese interpreter, questioned him. He was too frightened to talk. Wu spoke to him in the local dialect and in Mandarin, but though it was evident he understood, he remained silent and shook his head.

I took Wu and the doctor aside. "Prepare some sodium amytal," I said. "He'll talk."

The doctor grinned. "You'll never get a needle into that little devil," he said.

I called Tsu Fu and the Chinese guard. Wu explained the situation to them, whereupon they went into a huddle.

"What do they say?" I asked Wu.

"They say okay."

When I returned from the next room, the prisoner was quietly asleep, whatever method had been used to coerce him. The doctor was grinning and Tsu Fu was wiping his face with a cold towel. I then fed the questions to Wu, who translated to Tsu Fu, and he in turn spoke to the prisoner, the answers being relayed to me in the same complicated fashion.

At first, the prisoner was coy, as one is even under the influence of sodium amytal when facing severe punishment. He pretended not to understand Japanese and answered in the local Chinese dialect. When we exploded this, he pretended to be a Chinese agent and later a deserter from the Japanese. But after two hours of questioning and piecing together the answers, we learned that he had parachuted to the ground from a reconnaissance plane at night, carrying with him the sending device and other instruments. He wore typical coolie clothes — grass sandals, a dirty straw hat, faded blue pants, and soiled cotton shirt. On his person he carried a few thousand Chinese dollars.

When the Donkey, very excited and incoherent, turned up, the prisoner was asleep. I left him in the Donkey's care and reviewed what we had accomplished. Very little, really. Others would doubtless replace him. Either his capture would be made known in Hankow or guessed when he failed to broadcast at 6:00 P.M.

In my office over a second brandy with Wu, Tsu Fu, and the guard who had seized the spy, I was suddenly struck with an idea and cursed my earlier stupidity.

"Wu," I said, "we're going to broadcast to Hankow at six P.M."

"Have another drink," said Wu compassionately.

"No, I mean it. If we send a meteorological report each day, just as the spy did, and report low ceiling, the Japanese bombers will leave us alone. If the messages fail to come, Hankow will know something is wrong and drop another agent to send reports."

"He destroyed his code book."

"I don't need one. We've reconstructed enough of it for our purposes."

"It sounds screwy to me," Wu said. "Only yesterday you told the students that experienced operators could recognize signals from any given sender just as you recognize handwriting."

"That's so," I said. "Therefore, we'll make the spy send them. Come on, all of you; we'll go get the spy before he wakes up."

When we reached the doctor's, we were told the Donkey had taken the prisoner away an hour before.

In the car I said to Wu, "Tell the chauffeur to step on it."

At the prison there was much delay while Wu and Tsu Fu argued with the guards. Finally, they were admitted, and returned with an officer, who looked at me inquiringly. Wu went into a long harangue. Yes, the prisoner was there, the Donkey was there, and another general from headquarters.

"The Hatchet Man?" I asked.

"No, one of the Donkey's assistants."

"Well, what are we waiting for?"

"He says it is very irregular, but he'll take a chance."

Within, the officer looked in vain for the Donkey and then led us to the prisoner's cell. It was empty.

Wu cursed under his breath.

"The officer says maybe they are executing the prisoner."

"For Christ's sake!" I cried. "Have him stop it!"

Uncertain what to do, the officer led us at a snail's pace through a number of corridors and then into a large stone court. On the far side I recognized the Donkey and three other officers. And close to the wall, kneeling, his back to us, was the Japanese spy. At his head was the executioner, armed not with a Samurai sword but with a rifle.

I yelled to the Donkey, but my words were drowned by a

single shot. The prisoner slumped over, half his head blown off. Returning, I meditated on the Oriental mind and on the genius of W. S. Gilbert. Had he known the Donkey, he would, I believe, have married him off to Katisha, with her nice taste for prompt and gory executions. And serve them both jolly well right.

· Chungking, April 1939

IT HAS BECOME QUITE WARM NOW, though the sun still breaks through the mist of fog but seldom, and then only for a short time. Despite the fact that our prisoner was executed, we daily send three meteorological reports to Hankow. Visibility is always low at 6:00 A.M., so Hankow can scarcely be surprised that conditions are poor at that hour. But I can't believe they'll swallow low ceiling and visibility all the time. I do the sending and try to imitate our dead spy's touch, which I know well. It's improbable that I fool them, but they may be unsure, since the spy had no receiving set and Hankow cannot, therefore, ask questions. Now and then in the 6:00 P.M. report I give a high ceiling, but only when there is no moon. Leaving Hankow after 6:00 P.M. puts them here pretty late, for Hankow is five hundred miles away, so in reporting good bombing conditions at 6:00 P.M., I'm taking small risk. However, we are doubtless living in a fool's paradise.

Every day there are false alarms when the Japanese planes fly north through Szechuan to Chengtu and vicinity. The other day during one of these I was taking a siesta under my mosquito net in the hut when a Chinese pursuit plane crashed in my back yard. Rumor has it that the aviator, seeing a shadow, thought he was being pursued by a Japanese and bailed out, leaving the gunner to his fate in a crash landing. They had to dig him out. A fine mess.

The warmth that takes the kinks from my joints has brought

swarms of mosquitoes. Somehow hundreds get through my screens and at times cover the walls. The malaria mosquito, I am told, puts its head against the wall and sticks out its tail. If that is true, all these are malaria carriers. Every day I see some of my companions — a student, the chauffeur, an interpreter, a coolie — shaking with malaria.

I suggest that the Chinese as a race became yellow after suffering from this disease for thousands of years. Science should look into my hypothesis and name it after me. Lao Tsai has instructions to make the rounds of my hut every half-hour and swat the pests, but he is so incurably lazy that he never picks up a swatter until he sees me coming. At my office I have little trouble, because it is high above the outlying excrement pools and breeding places, with a breeze that discourages forays.

With all my care, as luck would have it, I laid myself open to infection the other night. April 13 was my birthday, and they gave me a party to celebrate the occasion. I *kam-peied* until 1:00 A.M. and was so tipsy when I got home that I threw off my clothes and lay down on my fancy silk box couch, instead of getting in bed under the mosquito netting. When I woke, I found an expensive wrist watch on my arm and my body covered with mosquito bites. Now I'm dosing myself with quinine and hoping for the best.

2

My adobe hut is becoming a rendezvous for Eurasians, nondescript Chinese, and foreign expatriates. I should like to know the stories of these people, the shifts of fortune that brought them here, and what may be their secret purposes. Probably I shall catch only glimpses and have to imagine the rest. It will be better that way, for I can then romanticize them a bit, whereas the pasts of some are probably sordid and possibly criminal. The numerous books I read about China, including those of Pearl Buck, did not prepare me for foreign society in

Chungking. As the lives of these folk touch mine, they will enter a little into these pages.

One group of four has a curiously complicated relationship. The young man is a Chinese who has recently returned from study in France. His divorced wife was a student in Russia. She is tuberculous, dresses in coolie clothes, though she tells me her father owns millions in real estate in North China, and is now on her way to nurse the Chinese wounded. She packs a gun twice the size of mine. When she calls on me, she is usually accompanied by her ex-husband's concubine, a charming person with foreign manners and hairdo. There is also a very pretty girl advertised as the daughter of the concubine, who is far too young for the role of parent, being no more than in her twenties. However, I call the concubine Mother, or, more familiarly, Mama, for she is clearly kin to the hot mamas of another land.

The young man recently went off to Saigon on some mission or other, or so he said, leaving his ex-wife fighting mosquitoes with burning punk sticks, and Mama and daughter alone to pursue their own devices. Mama, as I have remarked, is an attractive wench. She cannot read Chinese, but she is versed in foreign ways and with a few drinks of yellow wine performs esthetic dances for our entertainment. I was once told, and have no reason to disbelieve, that the girls of Washington, D.C., back home, eat more, drink more, and make love less than the girls of other American cities. So it is, seemingly, in Chungking. Chinese girls are natural gold diggers, and their men evidently encourage them to be so. As a visiting foreigner, I comply with the domestic customs. I had, now and then, gone horseback riding with Mama and daughter, and recently, acting on Mama's broad hint, I had them measured for riding habits. Since then, they have dropped in daily to learn when their clothes will be ready.

Last Monday Mama called at 10:00 A.M. and found me in bed. Monday morning is a time of rest for foreigners, because the whole of the Chinese people, or at least those controlled by the Central Party, gather on that day to venerate the memory of Sun Yat-sen, the father of their country. Rain or shine, hot or cold, my boys are assembled in a court each Monday and addressed by some party member. If the Generalissimo is in town, he frequently addresses the bigwigs in like fashion. The ceremony is conducted with the precise ritual of a religion, which indeed it is.

Not addicted to ritual, and knowing little Chinese, I was sound asleep on Monday when Lao Tsai came to tell me Mama was in the reception room. I put on a bathrobe and told him to bring her in, which he did, and we had fried eggs together. Most Chinese nibble at the white of a fried egg, leaving the yolk to the last. This they try to absorb in one mouthful at a single operation. The result is disastrous, with the yellow smearing their features and dripping onto the plate. Mama proved to be a delicate eater and quite won my affection.

She is an inveterate *mah-jong* player and gambles for high stakes with the wives and concubines of generals and the wealthy in the neighborhood. She is trying to teach me to play, not an easy task, since she speaks not a word of English and I little Chinese. Though Wu says that her accent is good and her Mandarin perfect, she cannot read Chinese ideographs. Consequently, when I look up a word in the English-Chinese dictionary and point to an ideograph, she can only shake her head and say, *"Pu tong."*

But her sign language is perfect and she had no trouble inquiring about her riding habit. I said, *"Mien tien"* — everything in China is "tomorrow" — and she was perfectly satisfied. After a few cups of yellow wine she gave up the task of teaching me *mah-jong* and turned on the gramophone, to which she tried to perform some of her acrobatic tricks. Chinese gowns, though slit high at the side, are not designed for gymnastic exercises. Mama therefore removed hers and performed with considerable grace while I played the gramophone to accompany her.

Tiring at last, she lay down on my box couch and motioned me beside her. Perhaps to make sure that she and Daughter got their riding habits, she thereupon removed the rest of her clothes and stretched out.

It was at this moment that she flinched with fright, and her eyes, fixed on the window across the room, grew big and round like doughnuts. It was semidark, for the windows are draped with heavy curtains. Even so, I could see through the screening a pair of hands that grasped the window ledge. Then a shaved head appeared. It was that of Fen Tao, my new chauffeur. He had climbed to the top of the bamboo structure that shelters my car; there was no other way he could see into the window, which is eight feet above the ground. Only Fen Tao, who hates all foreign devils, would show such contempt for my authority and position.

I do not share the Chinese feeling for coolies and servants, but Wu has taught me to demand of them the respect they show their Chinese masters. Servants and coolies are not permitted to use the same toilet, they cannot eat with their employers, and chauffeurs are not permitted to smoke while driving. But Fen Tao uses my bathtub — not that I give a damn — smokes while driving, which I don't object to, and delights in driving at breakneck speeds through crowded streets, because he knows the foreigner doesn't like to see people run down. A few days previously I had had Wu lecture him for reckless driving. To little effect, for the next day he knocked a child over in the street, fortunately without injury. I had him drive back to the house immediately, found an empty beer bottle, got back into the car, and told him I'd break it over his head unless he mended his ways.

Peeping is a common frailty, and I'm not above it myself, but Fen Tao's insolence had gone too far. As he blinked, endeavoring to see into the darkened room, I reached for my snub-nosed automatic, took careful aim at a hand grasping the window ledge, and fired. The hands slipped from the window ledge, and

Fen Tao, like the Monk of Siberia, disappeared with the "hell of a yell," his body crashing through the bamboo shelter. Loud screams and the hullabaloo of servants ensued. In a few moments the Donkey appeared, followed by Wu. The Donkey wished to make something of it, but Wu told him I should have killed the chauffeur instead of shooting off a finger. Mama was quite upset and kept pointing to her face, meaning, I suppose, that she would lose face. I think she will be consoled when the tailor delivers the riding habit. Meanwhile, I have got a new driver and won the respect of Wu, who thinks me, in general, far too easygoing in my ways.

· Chungking, May 1939

THE JAPANESE AT HANKOW, as I suspected, didn't fall for our faked meteorological reports very long and have presumably parachuted a couple of spies into the neighborhood to replace the dead weather reporter. Wireless cipher messages are sent out daily but at irregular intervals. These are doubtless on a prearranged schedule, which we will eventually dope out, but for the moment the irregularity makes it difficult to discover the position of the sender. Not knowing the sending time in advance, we cannot get our instruments in position. The messages are not in the cipher previously employed and are brief, taking only a few moments to send.

These preparations pointed toward trouble, which was not long in coming. During the afternoon of May 4, twenty-seven bombers raided us, starting a few fires, damaging the American embassy on the South Side, and killing a few hundred in downtown Chungking. Then on May 5 all hell broke loose.

We get advance telephone and wireless information of the approach of bombers into Szechuan, but we can't tell whether their objective is Chengtu, the downriver cities, or Chungking. On the 4th I stayed at the office during the raid, prepared to duck beneath the stone arch over the garden spring should the bombers fly directly overhead. Not that that would do much good, but one feels safer under something, if only a table. On the 5th I drove home with Ling and Wu.

We waited so long for the emergency to sound that we all fell asleep, to be awakened a couple of hours later by Lao Tsai yelling, *"Fei chi lai, fei chi lai."*

It was twilight, but our eyes, following the distant roar of the deep-throated engines, saw high in the northeast and beyond the city a number of silver birds glistening in the rays of the sun, now sunk below the horizon. We breathed easier, for if they followed their present course they would miss us by a safe margin. A little Chinese ragamuffin, unaware of his safety, crouched before us, whimpering and trembling, and clutched at our legs. No words or assurances would console him.

By car my hut seems far from the city, but the road describes a semicircle, and as a plane flies we are only five hundred yards from the city's ancient walls — far enough away if you keep your head, which is not easy to do. We were nervous but not too frightened until the planes veered slightly to the left along the Little River. Antiaircraft guns roared spasmodically, shooting little sparks followed by dark puffs that burst harmlessly beneath the bombers. The planes seemed to be flying directly toward us over the lower part of the city, sowing bright seeds of death that flowered in red clusters of flame, flashing as a watch ticks. Mushrooming geysers of smoke and debris leaped skyward, followed by the thunderous crashes of the exploding bombs. The earth heaved beneath our feet. From the city's tip at the confluence of the rivers the silver birds swept over the business section toward my office and the foreign embassies, the red flashes and the columns of debris rising in their path. Into the southwest they swept, over the Yangtze, and vanished beyond the mountains. Throughout Chungking a turbid wake of slow, creeping fires marked where they had passed.

We stood entranced by the cruel but magnificent scene, no one saying a word. Nor had we noted that the road nearby was cluttered with pedestrians, trucks, and rickshas. We did not at once realize that the Japanese bombers had slipped past our lookouts. Even the Chinese combat planes must have been grounded, for we had neither seen nor heard one. Was there treachery here? Chungking, within its ancient walls, is a triangle of no more than five square miles of brick and bamboo, an anthill housing a million souls. None had escaped underground. All were caught by surprise.

It was now wholly dark but for the conflagrations in the city whose skyward leaping flames cast a lurid and ghastly light.

"Let's get to the office," I said, hoping against hope my students had not been hit.

The roads were sure to be crowded, so we set out on foot by a short cut along the vegetable and rice-paddy terraces, cursing the stench and fighting mosquitoes. We came out on the highway just above the chateau and found to our relief that the fire was farther on, toward the German embassy. The chateau was safe.

The German embassy itself had been hit and the surrounding buildings were in flames. The embassy is built against the ancient wall, along which runs the city's water reservoir. This, fortunately, was intact, and the firemen, I thought, would have water.

Through an opening made in a wall by the explosion we could see numbers of coolies trapped by fire. The flames reached them. Then, mercifully for us, they were hidden from sight as the wall collapsed. I stood helpless, not knowing what to do. As a gesture I sent Wu back for the car, with instructions to help the streaming refugees who fought through the streets — to help as long as my small supply of gas would permit.

Ling and I pressed on and, by skirting fires and keeping to narrow side streets, succeeded in getting farther downtown. We reached the main thoroughfare again, only to find it jammed with the dead and the dying. One old fellow was sitting on the curb, his shirt ripped from his chest, moaning and muttering.

"What does he say?" I asked Ling.

"He says he wants to go home."

The old man struggled to his feet. His whole left side was torn open and we could see the heart beating. He took one step and fell dead.

Overhead, hanging on the electric wires strung to poles, was the body of a girl. Face and body seemed untouched, yet she was dead. Here a child's head lay in the gutter; there pieces of human bodies, crushed and broken. Columns of coolie stretcher bearers seemed everywhere, carrying away the wounded. The dead they brushed aside or trod underfoot. I looked on helplessly, knowing nothing of first aid, and neither, apparently, did the stretcher bearers.

"Where are they taking them?" I asked Ling.

"To the mission hospitals, perhaps."

We were now close to my friend's teahouse, which was in flames. Those who had escaped said my friend had been killed.

Coolie firemen with hand pumps and buckets of water lugged from the Little River and the Yangtze were risking their lives fighting the flames. Others were more hopefully dynamiting fire lanes, though to little purpose, it seemed, for the fires raged on.

At the silk shop where I had bought silks for my hut we met a bleeding clerk, whom Ling and I recognized. The shop had suffered a direct hit. The boss and his whole immediate family had sought shelter in the rear. This too had been hit and all had been killed.

The German House, home of George McKay, Fidelity's landlord, was surrounded by fires. Before the house, in the center of the street, was a bomb crater thirty feet deep. Three other bombs had only bracketed his house, fortunately for him, but had destroyed the buildings nearby. It seemed the fires might not reach him. Smoke, however, was coming from his windows. Here I might be useful, though I disliked having Ling know I was acquainted with George.

At the head of the stairs we found George, stripped to the waist, amid swirling smoke, cursing his servants as they threw sand and water on a fire that threatened to engulf his staircase. We both pitched in to help, and in an hour his building appeared safe, unless the adjoining fires broke out anew.

George wiped some of the grime from his face.

"Those goddamned Japs," he said. "Don't they know I'm a British subject!"

"How should they?" I laughed.

"I saw them coming!" he shouted. "I ran up the Union Jack, and look what they did to me!"

In the light of the burning houses and aided by flashlights, we made a tour of the house. The roof had been pierced in many places by flying stones, and one wing had been demolished. George's mumbled indignation at these outrages exploded into wrath when he examined his bedroom. The walls had been pierced in three places and the metal footpiece of his bed was dented. I picked up a flattened slug.

"They machine-gunned you," I said.

"The dirty bastards!" George cried. "How could they do this to me?"

The absurdity of the remark tickled me. The Japanese machine gunner flying low over the darkened city at two hundred miles an hour was hardly in a position to discriminate among targets or to know George's house from any other, despite the protective Union Jack. Nevertheless, George's words gave me pause. The Japanese had done this to him, who should have been safe. I remembered that Fidelity had warned me that George was employed by the Japanese, or at least had hinted as much. I liked George as an amusing person, but this was war, and something had to be done about him. My own security demanded it if he was found out.

On our way back to the hut, Ling and I circled the city's northern edge along the bank of the Little River. Here, too, appalling numbers had been killed. At the top of a flight of steps a dugout cut from soft stone had collapsed from a direct hit. Coolies were already at work, dragging out the bodies and laying them on the steps. Others threw them into coolie-drawn carts. The cave had been packed with refugees at the unexpected approach of the bombers. The bomb crater and the distorted naked bodies, from which the clothes had been clawed in the death struggle of suffocation, told the whole story all too plainly.

When we reached home it was daylight, and fires still swept the city. Wu was there with the chauffeur.

"What happened?" I asked.

"We took as many out of town as we could before we ran out of gas."

"Find the Donkey and get more," I ordered.

This, it appeared, they had tried unsuccessfully to do. I experienced a momentary hope that the Donkey had been a victim of the raid but sternly repressed it. Accident is seldom so providential.

"Let's all have a drink," I suggested.

Later we found the Donkey alive, as I had feared, secured more gas, and did what little we could to aid the evacuation of refugees. The Generalissimo ordered all government cars and trucks devoted to this purpose. For days the refugees streamed out of the city, amid clouds of dust, their little belongings tied to bamboo poles, children strapped to their backs. They filled the Chengtu Road and crowded into junks and sampans on the two rivers. The million people who had swarmed in the anthill of Chungking dwindled to a quarter of a million, among whom were five thousand dead and ten thousand wounded.

The city smoldered, to break out into fresh conflagrations when the bombers returned. It all seemed unreal, even with the mangled bodies of men and women and children before your eyes — unreal and unbelievable. There was the deep roar of the engines, scattered and futile antiaircraft fire, the sound of machine guns and explosions. There were bursts of flame, columns of smoke, rattling windows — all unreal, like some spectacle in a movie. Here the producer had put on a million-dollar Hollywood show. From behind the scene he called, "Camera, lights," and the camera began to turn. The sound technician synchro-

nized his sound effects. All very skillful, artificial, and inhuman
— a preview for the gods. Plotinus remarked that all life is but
shadow show, that the taking and sacking of towns and all the
agony of life are but a spectacle without reality. So, to the
unharmed bystander, seemed the bombing and burning of
Chungking. To one whose body was torn with bomb splinters,
it must have seemed otherwise.

2

After the big bombing we were on short rations at the chateau
for a time. Supplies from the country were interrupted, and
those we had we shared with the refugee children housed in the
Buddhist temple next door. I still had half a ton of canned food
that Ling had bought for me in Hong Kong, and this I dropped
at the mission hospital, where conditions were deplorable. I
sent Ling to interview my old eye doctor, thinking that he
would be the one to distribute the food wisely. Ling returned
with a long face.

"Your doctor isn't there," he said.

"Not there? Where is he?"

"He ran away with the others. Doctors afraid of bombs."

Upon further inquiry I learned that what Ling had said was
true. Few doctors remained in Chungking, and these were
mostly from the mission hospitals and the English and American gunboats. Yet there were ten thousand wounded in the city.

I said to Ling, "Foreign doctor would be afraid, too, but
more afraid to run. He'd be afraid of what people say."

"Chinese doctor honest," said Ling. "He afraid and he run."

Ling was neither surprised at or ashamed of his people. Nor
should I have been surprised, for the government states openly
in the newspapers that China had only five thousand college
graduates each year and that these are far too valuable to risk
at the front. The Generalissimo's two sons, one his own and one
adopted, are variously reported in Berlin, Paris, and America,
dancing with white women while their country bleeds slowly to
death.

I said to Wu and Ling, "Can you imagine General Lee's sons gadding around abroad during the Civil War? They fought, and at the front, too."

Ling wasn't impressed, and Wu, educated in Honolulu, said, "How about President Lincoln's son? He went to Harvard while Lincoln sent other Northern boys to their death. Lincoln's son didn't fight. In fact, Lincoln asked Grant as a friend to give him a special post."

Wu probably knew his history better than I, and in Chungking I had no books for reference. I shifted my position to safer ground.

"Well, you must admit, if you know so much American history, that by and large the middle- and upper-class boys die on the battlefield. But I have yet to hear of a Chinese upper- or middle-class boy smelling gunpowder, much less dying on the field."

"Adviser," Ling said, "you do not understand Chinese custom and way of thought. Ancient Wisdom says, 'good iron not made for nail; good man not made for soldier.' "

Knowing I was licked, I changed the subject.

"Tell the Donkey for me that those Japanese planes could have slipped through our outposts only by treachery."

"I hear three were murdered," Wu said.

"Exactly. Suggest to the Donkey that all outposts go in pairs."

This was well enough and should impress the Donkey with my alertness. But I still didn't like George's presence in Chungking. Should the Donkey investigate him, the fact that I had been friendly with him might come out. George's absurd complaint about the Japanese bombing his house and shooting him up, and his use of the English flag, all gave promise of trouble. Besides, I liked George and didn't want him seized as a spy. I suggested to Wu and Ling that it would be best for George, and us too, if George was got away.

"You think he's a spy?" Wu asked.

"Not a dangerous one," I said, "but a nuisance."

"You want us to do what?"

"Force him to leave Chungking. Chinese coolies are superstitious, as you know. Suggest to the old beggar who commands George's district that George must be a spy, because the Japanese missed George's building and destroyed all the buildings adjoining. Then word will get around."

Wu and Ling agreed that my talk was good medicine and presumably acted on it. A few days later I dropped in on George.

"I'm leaving for Shanghai," he said, "and I want to thank you again for helping to fight the flames."

"Business, George?"

"No. I'm sick of these Chinese. You know what my girl said? Said I was a Japanese spy. Her father wouldn't let me in his house. He spat on me and called me a spy."

"But why did he do that, George?"

"Why? The damned fools say I'm a spy because my place didn't burn down. Everywhere they spit at me."

I agreed that his was a hard case.

"Chinese are simple people, George. It might be dangerous to remain, however mistaken they are."

"I know," he said. "I'm going tomorrow. Flying out to Hong Kong and then going to Shanghai. My daughters are there. I'll be glad to get home. Chungking stinks."

"It sure does, George," I agreed, and shook hands with him.

• *Chungking, June 1939*

*I*T HAS BECOME REALLY HOT, temperature from 95 to 110 degrees and humidity up to 96. I can judge the latter by the number of drops of water per minute that drip from my nose and chin or by the streams of water on my walls. My poor *amah* washes three complete changes each day — socks, shirts, underwear, white suits — and even so, I am wet most of the time. At the office one fan blows on me all the time, and at home I have three, two in my sitting room and one in my bedroom. At night I sleep behind mosquito netting on a finely woven bamboo mat, for cotton mats are too hot to sleep on. My pillow is of some soft native grass. The fan plays on me all night.

If no bombers show up, my routine is to arrive late at the office, enjoy luncheon and a siesta from one to three in the afternoon, and then return to the office for a while. I have dinner at home and then go downtown for a few glasses of vile Chinese white wine, a shave, a game of billiards, or the like — anything to kill time. Later in the evening, because I then concentrate better, I work alone, often as late as 3:00 or 4:00 A.M. After seeing lights in my rooms so late at night, the Donkey wrote me a nice memorandum as a peace offering. Translated, it reads:

Honorable Adviser:
You are working much too hard, so you should, I think, spend
Sundays at least on the South Bank, where I have engaged riding

horses for you and your guards. You will find it cooler, for there are many shaded paths. In no circumstances should you go without protection.

Faithfully yours, etc., etc.

Ling, Wu, and I — without the guards — tried it last Sunday. The horses are gentle and about the size of Shetland ponies, sturdy little beasts capable of climbing rocky terraces. We rode to the top of the First Range, and on the way back, seeing a foreigner in shorts enter a compound, we dismounted and followed him into what proved to be the Chungking Club. Here we met the president, a Eurasian, and a heavyset, red-faced American named Schwer, who is one of the officers and was happy to meet another American. He owns a small ice plant in Chungking and lives near the Yangtze on the North Bank, close to the confluence of the two rivers. Since the club bar accepts no cash, he arranged that I should sign chits in his name and promised to put me up for membership. The members are officers of the American gunboat moored to the river bank just below the club, the personnel of the foreign embassies, a few foreign advisers and Chinese Maritime Tax employees, and other nondescript exiles.

The next day I was surprised to find that our Eurasian friend was manager of an import-export firm on the South Bank. Ling and I had gone to clear a speculative shipment of American cigarettes, coffee, and gin, which an American friend of mine in Hong Kong had sent to me. The goods had been consigned in a truck that the firm had bought from him. Through a misunderstanding, part had been sent in the name of Herbert Yardley and part in the name of Herbert Osborn. I had the papers for both shipments and explained to the Eurasian that Herbert Yardley was in the country and that I was his authorized agent. The Eurasian looked politely skeptical, and I could scarcely blame him.

We paid the freight and customs duties for the entire consignment and had coolies carry it to my hut in Chungking. The cost of the goods in Chinese money was $6000 at the time of purchase three months ago, and the value now at wholesale prices in Chungking is $12,000 — a paper profit of $6000 Chinese, which I am splitting with Ling and Wu. They are good boys and have served me well. They would not accept money from me, but in this way I reward them and let them save face. The $2000 each receives is as much as they earn in a year. My own paper profit is illusory, for the original outlay of $6000 Chinese cost me $600 in gold, and because of the rapid increase in the price of gold, my $8000 Chinese is now worth but $535 gold — a net loss of $65. In other words, inflation more than keeps pace with profits. As a businessman, I don't look so hot. However, in the long run I still hope to beat these Chinese Shylocks, with their 20 percent interest rates, at their own banking game.

A few days after I met Schwer, he sent me a chit inviting me to dinner. He has the entire top floor of a five-story compound, a nice apartment with a veranda running the length of the building and overlooking the Yangtze. I made him a present of a bottle of imported gin — lessening my paper profits by $100 — which we drank before dinner, with the help of a Dutch adviser to the Bank of China and his petite Chinese mistress, who spoke a few words of English.

After dinner we sat on the screened veranda in the warm twilight and watched the river darken while the native oil lamps on the junks and sampans blinked like fireflies. Then the scene was slowly flooded with amber light, and a full moon peered over the First Range, beyond the river. The alert sirens presaging a bombing raid sounded almost immediately.

The Dutchman and his mistress left quickly to anticipate the rush across the river for safety. Schwer produced a bottle of homemade gin, a concoction of Chinese alcohol used as fuel for buses, boiled river water, and synthetic juniper drops. To this we added the product of his own factory, a poplike drink manufactured of charged water and synthetic flavoring. This mixture was somewhat improved by the addition of real ice. I at once subscribed to one of Schwer's homemade iceboxes and daily deliveries of ice, though the deliveries, I found shortly, meant that you picked it up yourself.

"They'll be here in a couple of hours," Schwer said. "We may as well fortify ourselves."

"Here's to crime," I said, lifting my glass.

"That's a new one on me," Schwer said, taking a drink. "What crime?"

"It's an Indiana toast, no doubt stolen from somewhere. It goes, 'Here's to crime.' Then you're supposed to answer 'And may we all be hanged for rape.' If the toast is to a girl and she answers appropriately, the first one says, 'If rape is imminent, relax.' "

"A nice sentiment." Schwer nodded approvingly and choked, as I had done, on the synthetic alcohol. "Better," he added somberly, "than slow death on the Yangtze."

I asked after a moment, "How long since you were home?"

"Nearly thirty years," he said.

It was a terrifying thought.

"I'll never go back," he added. "I wouldn't know what to do." He poured another drink.

To change the subject, I asked, "Where do you go during raids?"

"To a cave nearby. Want to go along?"

"No, I'm afraid of caves. My mother punished me by locking me in closets."

"Caves are hell," Schwer said. "And the goddamned Chinese guards won't let you talk. The other day one yelled at us to be quiet. He said the planes could hear us. Where do you go?"

"Oh, any place or no place. If I haven't had much to drink, I drive out the Chengtu Road. If I've had a few, I go to bed in my hut and fall asleep."

"You like your place?"

"It's good enough. But I want a more varied diet. I planted

some imported tomato seeds, but when they came up, the clay choked them to death. I'm thinking of buying a cow for milk and some chickens for fresh eggs. This hot weather spoils everything before it arrives from the country."

Schwer regarded me with mild pity.

"You're nuts," he said. "The cow won't give any milk, the servants will steal the eggs, and the rats will eat the chickens."

"But I can try. I want to bottle some tomato juice for next winter, too."

"You'll soon learn the futility of trying anything in China," Schwer said morosely. "I tried to bottle tomato juice myself, but the Chinese are so dirty that all the caps blew off the bottles. But seeing is believing. I'll give you some bottles and caps if you want to try it."

The drink had affected him and he looked drunk. Quite suddenly he became quarrelsome and berated the two houseboys, whom he had caught eavesdropping. He slapped one and knocked the other down.

"They don't understand what we say," I protested.

"Sure they do. The Chinese government sets them to spy on me. My two good boys ran away at the first bombings. I'm trying these boys out. I hit them, and if they don't run away I know they're spies."

This system of testing and retaining servants intrigued me, and I countered with the story of Mama and the chauffeur, which so pleased him that he put the bottle of bus fuel aside and opened a bottle of imported Scotch. We were now on such amiable terms that I ventured to ask what the Chungking Club committee had done about my application for membership.

"That goddamned Eurasian blackballed you," Schwer said. "I'm going to make an issue of it," he added darkly.

"I'd rather you wouldn't," I said, not wishing my business in China too closely looked into.

Schwer laughed and winked slyly. "I told him you were someone important or you wouldn't be running around in a government car. I hope you sell them a bill of goods, but don't forget the ten percent squeeze if you want to do business."

So that's what they say about me, I thought. Big munitions salesman. But that surely wouldn't explain the Eurasian black-balling me.

"What's the Eurasian got against me?" I asked.

"He said you were going by two names, and a man with two names must have something to hide." He emptied his glass and poured another. "I told the yellow sonofabitch that any American could join if he wanted to, no matter if he had ten names."

The pleasant fog of drink and good-fellowship was dispelled by the shriek of the emergency siren. That banshee wail strikes me cold sober in three seconds.

"I'd better get to my car," I said, "before the chauffeur deserts me."

"I'm getting out myself," said Schwer. "Drop in again. And don't forget to try my system on your servants. If they run away, they're okay. If they stay, they're paid to watch you."

· Chungking, July 1939

LIFE IN CHUNGKING GOES ON much as usual, despite the bombings and evacuation. After dark on moonless nights one of the three movie houses that still stand and two of the innumerable sing-song theaters are open for business. For each tea shop destroyed by bombs or fires, another springs up. There is also one poolroom, where I often go to play Chinese three-ball billiards with a young Chinese who speaks a few words of English. He gambles at billiards and *mah-jong* for a living. He usually beats me at billiards. *Mah-jong* I do not play — seemingly I am too dumb to grasp it. He was in love with a sing-song girl whom he wished to marry. It cost him $5000 Chinese to buy her freedom from the *amah,* who in turn had purchased her from river coolies at an early age and trained her. Now she is with him all the time, and when I remarked that I must have contributed most of the $5000 that was the price of her freedom, both giggled happily. She, too, speaks a few words of English, and I call her Marguerite, for what reason I don't know. The last time I saw the husband he took me to the rear and handed me a sealed Chinese envelope. There was no superscription. I asked him where he got it, but he would not say — just told me to open it later in secret.

It was from Fidelity. I could scarcely credit it. She must be insane to return to Chungking now that there is a price on Wang Ching-wei's head. She asked me to come to South Springs the following Sunday and meet her at a small hotel after dark.

I took no chances on being followed. While everyone was enjoying his Sunday siesta, I drove away by myself, using the ignition key I had secretly made some months before. Fidelity's room was on the second floor at the corner overlooking the bath houses. A native oil lamp lit the hallway, but dimly. Her door opened as I approached. I was wringing wet with perspiration, but she seemed cool enough, dressed in colored silk lounging pajamas and foreign-made slippers. Her haircut was a boyish bob with bangs in front, and she looked very youthful and very pretty, too.

Cautioning me to silence, she led me to a wicker bamboo settee, gave me a fan, and sat beside me. Two Chinese lamps smoked and flickered in a far corner of the room. It was all very Oriental and mysterious and a shade ominous.

"You don't seem very happy to see me," she said in a low voice.

"I'm happy," I said, "but I'm scared, too."

"For me or yourself?"

"For you, of course," I said politely — and untruthfully.

"Well, you needn't be."

She seemed confident enough, and I was puzzled.

"There's a price on Wang's head."

"Yes." She smiled.

"And you're one of his concubines."

"Yes."

"But in no danger?"

"No-o — not much. Not more than you. Not more than many of us."

I disliked being classed with the many of us. I removed my coat and wiped the perspiration from my arms, head, and face. She lighted cigarettes for both of us and said, "I brought some French cognac with me. I'll get glasses."

While she was gone I looked about the room. It was the usual thing in interior China — bare floors and walls, no curtains or shades. The windows were screened, but a few mosquitoes buzzed here and there nonetheless. Through the bamboo portière I could see the adjoining room, furnished with a bamboo bed canopied with mosquito netting.

Fidelity returned with two glasses and a bottle and poured us drinks. As I drank mine I slapped at my ankles. "Don't these damned things bite you?" I asked.

She laughed. "You foreigners are soft. I'll light some incense." She placed a piece in each window and another at our feet. The lazy curls of smoke filled the room with their fragrance.

"Am I still a riddle?" she asked.

"Yes," I said and walked about the room, thinking. Though I had not seen him, I knew the Hatchet Man had been back for ten days. Could she, too, be in his employ? It was possible. And if she reported only to him and he had been absent on the night of Wang's escape, would that explain her actions toward me?

"How long have you been here?" I asked abruptly.

"Oh, a week or so."

"Why did you come back?"

She smiled. "You're thinking I came to see you?"

"Do I look that dumb?" I said.

"Well, you needn't be so sour about it."

I sat beside her again.

"Fidelity," I said, "do you know General — — " and I gave the Hatchet Man's name.

"Who doesn't," she replied lightly. "Let's talk of something pleasant." She rose to refill our glasses. "There isn't much time. I'm flying to Hong Kong Wednesday night."

"You're joining Wang again?"

"Perhaps."

"Why don't you poison him and have done with it?" I suggested.

"Maybe I will." She laughed.

"You're leaving Wednesday. So how about a dinner party Tuesday night — a private affair?"

"How private?"

"There's an English-speaking Chinese chap here who has

taken a liking to me. My interpreters call him the One-Armed Bandit. He has something to do with antiaircraft fire. He's an expert artillery officer and an ex-bandit, so they say. Lost an arm in combat, he tells me, but more likely by an assassin's bullet. However that may be, he sometimes takes me to his battery during a raid. I like to watch the lights on the bombers at night and hear his antiquated guns roar. They never seem to hit anything, but they make a pleasing noise."

"I know who you mean," Fidelity said, "but he's not an ex-bandit. He's still active."

"Sure, I know that," I said with a laugh.

The One-Armed Bandit is famous throughout China for his lawlessness. The story goes that he kidnapped Chinese girls from the convents in Shanghai and sold them to Japanese generals after he was through with them. Even in Chungking he seizes any girl he fancies and has her brought to his chateau — the whole affair hushed by money. He is in league with the governor of Szechuan Province, who has two divisions of troops he refused to send to the front. These live off the fat of the land and defy the Generalissimo, even though at times they are billeted only thirty miles away.

I said to Fidelity, "A girl he knows in Hong Kong is flying up to see him on Monday. He invited me to dinner for Tuesday night. There were to be just the three of us, but he said I could invite someone if I liked. How about it? Would he recognize you? He came here after you left."

"No," she said and looked at me appraisingly. "But there is something back of this. What is it?"

"I simply wanted to see you again and be agreeable," I protested.

"You can see me here again if you like. Anyhow, you don't have to be agreeable."

It was clear I would have to be open with her.

"Very well, then. I think if you go you may be able to help me out with something. But it may be dangerous."

III

She was instantly alert.

"Just what is it you want me to do?"

"I'll tell you the whole story," I said, and while I talked, she smoked and frowned.

2

On Tuesday evening I succeeded as before in escaping alone with the car and met Fidelity not far from Wang Lung Men. From there we drove to the One-Armed Bandit's home on the Chengtu Road, which runs along the Little River.

What I wanted Fidelity to do will be intelligible only in the context of Chinese life and my official work in unraveling wireless intercepts. Graft and treachery are not unknown in the United States, but we assume, and rightly, that not many citizens would deliberately sell out their country. In China it is different. Whereas we had one Benedict Arnold, in China the Benedict Arnolds are numberless. I once heard the London *Times* correspondent say, after seeing a Chinese spy drama with an all-Chinese cast, "It's remarkable how well Chinese actors portray the part of spies and traitors." Art has here only to hold the mirror up to nature.

We in the Chinese Black Chamber had for long suspected the One-Armed Bandit of being the chief of our local traitors. He openly used the wireless of one of the Szechuan infantry divisions billeted close to Chungking to exchange messages in code with friends in Shanghai. Though the names were camouflaged, we knew who they were. In the first of my interviews with the Hatchet Man I had been ordered to concentrate on these intercepts. This we had done, but thus far with no success. The code messages of other generals we had in some cases deciphered and found a few that revealed treachery. Purges, we learned through the grapevine, had ensued, though we were never so informed officially.

The Bandit's messages had resisted all our attacks. They were sent in four-figure groups, such as 1349, 5727, 7234, and the like.

Analysis indicated change each day. Thus, if a group of four figures occurred often on one date, indicating that it was a common ideograph, the same group might not appear at all in a message of later date. The key, it seemed, was altered daily. How then go about deciphering the messages?

Curiously enough, the simplest wireless or telegram in Chinese must be sent in code, because the Chinese language cannot be reduced to a few letters, as can English, German, Russian, and many other languages. Nor can it be reduced to *kana,* like Japanese. Even such a message in Chinese between husband and wife as "Will arrive tomorrow night" must be converted to code before transmission. The sender goes to a telegraph office and encodes his message from a ten-thousand-ideograph Chinese public code book that he finds there. The code book is nothing more than a Chinese dictionary of the ten thousand most common Chinese words or ideographs, including, of course, numerals and radicals. The first word is represented by 0000, the second by 0001, the third by 0002, and so on, up to 9999. The sender converts his message into these numerals, hands it to the telegraph operator, who transmits it to its destination, where the process is reversed and the message decoded into its original form. (A page of this code book or dictionary, on sale throughout the world and universally used by the Chinese, is shown opposite.)

Though we believed the Bandit was using this book, we thought he also scrambled the figure groups after his message was encoded. For example, the first group of his message might be 9345, but he would change it perhaps to 1748 so that when we looked up 1748 in the code book it made no sense.

His messages, however, had one other characteristic. The first group of each message was five letters, like *miteo* or *lofed,* followed by figure groups, like 9345, 3847, 6472, and so on. These first five letters intrigued me, and I had given much study to them, often lying awake at night trying to read them. Long

13 15	16 19	17 21				3 5	4 5	5	5 6 · 09 · 30 32
0900 噶 KA	0910 囂 YIN	0920 嚼 CHIAO CHÜEH	0930 叻 LI	0940 困 CHÜN	0950 圇 LUN	0960 土 T'U	0970 坋 FEN	0980 坡 P'O	0990 垌 CHIUNG
0901 嗉 NUNG	0911 嚲 TO ×	0921 囀 CHUAN	0931 口 WEI	0941 囹 LING	0951 圂 HUN HUAN	0961 在 TSAI	0971 均 CHÜN	0981 坤 K'UN	0991 坳 AO
0902 囈 HUI YÜEH	0912 韉 CH'AN	0922 囁 CHE NIEH	0932 回 HUI	0942 固 KU	0952 圔 YU	0962 圬 YÜ	0972 坊 FANG	0982 坦 T'AN	0992 型 HSING
0903 囤 TUN	0913 囐 YEN	0923 囂 HSIAO	0533 囚 CH'IU	0943 囿 YU	0953 圍 WEI	0963 圩 WU	0973 坿 T'AN	0983 坭 NI	0993 垓 KAI
0904 囉 CHÜEH	0914 囀 P'IN	0924 囊 JANG	0934 四 SZU	0944 囨 P'U	0954 園 YÜAN	0964 圭 KUEI	0974 坎 K'AN	0984 坵 CH'IU ×	0994 垝 KUEI
0905 嚀 NING	0915 嚮 HSIANG	0925 囉 LO	0935 囟 CH'UAN TS'UNG	0945 圄 YÜ	0955 圓 YÜAN	0965 圮 P'I	0975 坏 P'EI	0985 坷 K'O	0995 垠 YIN
0906 嚅 JU	0916 譽 K'U ×	0926 囊 NANG	0936 囚 YIN	0946 圈 CHÜAN CH'ÜAN	0956 圖 T'U	0966 地 TI	0976 坐 TSO	0986 坼 CH'E	0996 垢 KOU
0907 嚇 HO HSIA	0917 嚴 YEN	0927 囈 I	0937 囷 TUN T'UN	0947 圉 YÜ	0957 團 T'UAN	0967 圻 CH'I	0977 坑 K'ENG	0987 垂 CH'UI	0997 垣 YÜAN
0908 嚏 T'I	0918 嚨 LUNG	0928 囑 CHU	0938 困 K'UN	0948 國 KUO	0958 圜 HUAN YÜAN	0968 址 CHIH	0978 坂 PAN	0988 坪 P'ING	0998 垞 CH'A ×
0909 嚙 NIEH	0919 嚶 YING	0929 囓 NIEH	0939 囝 HU	0949 圅 HAN	0959 圙 T'U	0969 坻 CH'IH TI ×	0979 坌 P'EN P'EN ×	0989 坫 TIEN	0999 垤 TIEH ×

厂ㄙ又（口口土）土夂夂

series of these letters were embedded in my mind. I could lie in the darkness and study them.

Though I have pages of matter, I quote as illustrations only the first five letter groups from the messages sent between June 1 and June 15.

t	i	t	t	h	(Sent	June	1st)
b	v	e	b	n	"	"	2nd
p	s	i	p	n	"	"	3rd
c	d	t	c	h	"	"	4th
a	t	o	a	u	"	"	5th
h	r	o	h	t	"	"	6th
w	t	l	w	i	"	"	7th
t	w	n	t	d	"	"	8th
p	i	s	p	i	"	"	9th
g	d	d	u	g	"	"	10th
e	w	w	e	e	"	"	11th
e	h	e	e	r	"	"	12th
i	l	g	i	h	"	"	13th
r	g	i	r	n	"	"	14th
s	o	e	s	d	"	"	15th

If I could unravel these letter groups, I felt sure I would be on the road to discovering the meanings of the body itself. Late in June, as I was lying on my couch one night during an impending raid, thinking not at all of ciphers but cursing myself for coming to China, a faint glimmering of truth flashed to mind. Sometimes I had fallen asleep before the bombers came and as a precaution had placed pillows over my vital organs, leaving all three fans blowing to keep me comfortable. As I was lying thus the letters danced in my mind.

The letter group E W W E E sent on June 11 had always intrigued me. Was the doublet E E significant? Could E E perchance equal 11 — the 11th of June?

If so, the entire group would equal E W W E E. Perhaps,

1 ? ? 1 1

I thought, the first three letters equal the number of the message and the last two the date. If so, the group G D D U G, sent on the 10th, would read G D D U G. In my mind I placed the

         0 ? ? 1 0

tentative decipherments one above the other:

    0 ? ? 10 sent June 10
    1 ? ? 11 sent June 11

The answer was so electrifying that I failed to notice, despite the heat, that the fans had died, signaling that the power line had been cut off at the near approach of bombers. I had indeed been stupid. Here, I said to myself, are two three-figure groups, presumably consecutive, the first beginning with 0 and ending in a doublet, the second beginning with 1 and also ending in a doublet,

    G D D
    0 ? ?

    E WW
    1 ? ?

There can be only one answer, 099 and 100. The complete decipherments are, without doubt,

    G D D U G
    0 9 9 1 0 (Number 99 sent June 10)

    E WWE E
    1 0 0 1 1 (Number 100 sent June 11)

In the excitement of my discovery my mind was closed to my surroundings, but now, back to earth, as I moved to get pad and pencil for further analysis I could hear the deep-throated roar of Japanese bombers overhead.

They must be after the electric light plant only two hundred yards distant, I thought, and covered my face and body with pillows. But I could not drown out the terrifying scream of descending bombs. The rush of air from the first explosion tore open my door and showered me with plaster from the ceiling. Crashes were all around me. Then a splitting explosion deafened me, sucked the air from my lungs, and hurled me across the room, glass and timber raining upon me.

I lay stunned for a few moments, got my breath, and crawled out, none the worse, it seemed, except for a few scratches on my bald head. But ciphers were definitely knocked from my brain. Instead, I thought of a drink, but when I examined what was left of my closet containing ten cases of imported gin, I found a sickening clutter of broken bottles. Out of ten cases I recovered intact just seven bottles — all imported from distant Hong Kong.

I took one and climbed through the rubble to the street, opened it to steady my nerves, and sat down on a stone to await the return of Wu, Ling, and the chauffeur, who had driven out the Chengtu Road.

I idly watched my two dozen hens, released by bombs from the pen nearby, cackling from fear, I gathered, for they never to my knowledge laid an egg. Could it be that the constant explosions broke the unhatched eggs? More likely my houseboy stole them.

I beguiled the time on the curbstone by drinking gin from the bottle and contributing to the Ancient Wisdom as it treats of eggs and servants. Thus:

In a house with many servants, the hens lay few eggs.
   or
He who would eat eggs must gather them with his own hands.
   or
An egg in the pan is worth two in the pen.
   or

From the old Chinese ideograph "to fire," meaning by easy analogy "to cook," we have the pithy epigram

To fire egg, first fire servant.

I seem to have forgotten the wise sayings composed during the second third of the bottle, which is a loss to literature.

It was almost dusk when the car came back. Ling and Wu gazed on the ruins with long faces.

"I'll stay with Schwer for a while," I said. "Don't look so glum. We'll find another home."

Fortunately, we had sold the small cargo of merchandise, except the gin, which I had so unwisely saved for myself. My fine radio was beyond repair, at least beyond repair in China. We were digging out some of my clothes from the debris when the Donkey came. He looked very angry. "What's he squawking about?" I asked.

"He says Number One will imprison him if you get hurt."

"I didn't know my skin was so valuable."

"He says you're supposed to drive to country to go in caves when bombers come."

"Okay," I said. "I've had my lesson. Tell him I need another radio."

"He says you should sleep at the office. You can use the one there."

"Not me," I said. "I'm a free man now." We gathered up the bottles and dusted off some of my clothing. I was tired and hungry, and I knew Schwer would feed me.

He didn't seem too happy to see me, for with him was the Dutch adviser's girl, and it appeared that I had interrupted a party. But when he saw my gin, he cheered up. I told him I'd lost my home. He gave me a room, and after I had washed off some of the grime, I joined them on the veranda. I spoke rapidly so that the Chinese girl would not understand.

"Where's the Dutchman?" I asked.

"He ran away. He can't take bombings."

"And you took care of his possessions."

"She is nice, isn't she?"

"How much does she cost you a month?"

"Three hundred. Inflation's here." He looked dreamily into the past. "I've had better for less."

"You have to feed her?" I asked.

"Sure. You should get yourself a girl."

"Not if I have to feed her," I said.

Chinese cooks are never embarrassed by the arrival of unexpected guests, because they always cook four times too much to ensure enough for themselves and distant relatives. At dinner Schwer grinned at me and asked, "How's the egg business?"

"I have, or at least had, two dozen hens but no eggs."

"And your cow?"

"The cow gives no milk. So I subscribed for milk from a Chinese across the river. But I gave that up too when he delivered it in an old beer bottle with a dirty paper stopper. I think it was mostly soy-bean juice, anyway."

"Just as I thought." Schwer chuckled. "And the tomato juice business?"

"I didn't have much luck," I admitted sadly. "It all went to vinegar, and as you said, the caps all blew off. Now if you want the whole picture, ask me about the fruit business."

"Well, how about it?"

"I put up twenty half-gallon jars of peaches in these Chinese jars with lids covered with water to keep out the air. The water evaporated, my houseboy failed to renew it, and the peaches all turned to mold."

"Cheer up," he said. "I'll give you a five-gallon jar of sour pickles. Nothing hurts sour pickles. Not even Chinese filth."

The girl, whose name is Elaine, she says, given to her by missionaries, spoke in Szechuan Chinese.

"What does she say?" I asked.

Schwer got up from the table and put a waltz record on his gramophone. "She wants to dance," he said.

For a cordial he poured out some green sweet stuff, made, I suspected, from the Chinese bus fuel oil that Schwer used as a base for all his drinks. After watching Schwer and Elaine take a drink of it and not fall dead on the spot, I tried a cautious snifter myself. It was terrible and tasted like embalming fluid. But it restored the chain of thought interrupted by the bombing raid, and taking a pencil and some paper, I retired to my room.

The gramophone scratched on and on and I could hear laughter. But as I began to write out the beginnings of messages I had been mentally studying, the music and laughter faded. Starting from the group E W W E E, the decipherment of which I had thought to be No. 100, 11th, I worked backward and forward, filling in the message numbers and the dates, so that the decipherments read from Message No. 90, dated the 1st, to Message No. 104, dated the 15th:

```
tit  th
090  01

bve  bn
091  02

psi  pn
092  03

cdt  ch
093  04

ato  au
094  05

hro  ht
095  06

wtl  wi
096  07

twn  td
097  08

pis  pi
098  09

gdd  ug
099  10
```

eww ee
100 11

ehe er
101 12

ilg ih
102 13

rgi rn
103 14

soe sd
104 15

It is an axiom in my profession that a decipherment itself
may reveal little of the why's and wherefore's, but that once the
decipherments are reduced or converted to the original sequences, the resultant behaviors may give a clue. I therefore
wrote out the normal sequence 0 1 2 3 4 5 6 7 8 9 and placed
the decipherments beneath. Taking the first group,

T I T T H, I had this,
0 9 0 0 1

0 1 2 3 4 5 6 7 8 9
t h   i

In other words, 0 equals t, 1 equals h, and 9 equals i. The
meanings for 2 3 4 5 6 7 8 are unknown. Treating the second
group B V E B N in the same fashion, I had,
       0 9 1 0 2

0 1 2 3 4 5 6 7 8 9
b e n   v

That is, 0 equals b, 2 equals n, 9 equals v, and the meanings
for 3 4 5 6 7 8 are unknown.

Using this procedure, I made the following chart:

0 1 2 3 4 5 6 7 8 9
t h   i

```
0 1 2 3 4 5 6 7 8 9
b e n         v

0 1 2 3 4 5 6 7 8 9
p   i n       s

0 1 2 3 4 5 6 7 8 9
c     t h       d

0 1 2 3 4 5 6 7 8 9
a     o u       t

0 1 2 3 4 5 6 7 8 9
h       o t     r

0 1 2 3 4 5 6 7 8 9
w         l i   t

0 1 2 3 4 5 6 7 8 9
t           n d w

0 1 2 3 4 5 6 7 8 9
p             s i

0 1 2 3 4 5 6 7 8 9
g u             d

0 1 2 3 4 5 6 7 8 9
w e
```

I stopped at this point, my pulse mounting as I saw the results. Taking the digraph decipherments in their order, I had this:

```
th
be
in
th
ou
ot
li
nd
```

```
si
gu
we
```

Every one of these digraphs is frequent in the English language. I quickly rearranged the rest of the groups:

```
0 1 2 3 4 5 6 7 8 9
h e r
```

```
0 1 2 3 4 5 6 7 8 9
l i g h
```

```
0 1 2 3 4 5 6 7 8 9
g r   i n
```

My heart stood still as I saw whole words emerge:

```
her
ligh?
gr?in
```

If the question marks are filled in, the words are

```
her
light
grain or groin
```

Why is this? What method of encipherment would produce these results? Why do words emerge? Why are the initial letters, those under the numeral 0, common *initial* letters of English words? Experience gives the answer: *The cipher is based on the first lines of different pages of an English text.*

It all seemed simple now. The One-Armed Bandit encoded his messages in the public Chinese code book. His having such a code book in his possession would not excite suspicion, because the code book is common property, necessary to Chinese if they use the wireless or telegraph. Then he disguised the four-figure code groups by changing the figures to others, using the same page of English text used to encipher the message number and date. And this English book, to allay suspicion, would doubtless be a common one, a book that might well be found in any small library or possessed by an English-reading Chinese. The method is simple. To explain, I take a line from a book before me:

> It was dusk when the priest came.

The ten numerals are written below this:

> It was dusk when the priest came.
> 01 234 56 7   89

The repeated letters in the key, s and w, are skipped to avoid more than one meaning. Employing these values, Message No. 90, June 1, would appear in cipher as:

> 0 8 0 0 1
> i hi i t

The method of determining the pages to be used for the key must, of course, be arranged in advance by correspondents. In this case I took page 7, the sum of 6 (June is the 6th month) and 1 (1st). But the method of selecting pages is infinite.

Of course this is not all. From someplace on this page, letters will be selected to determine a *figure* cipher to encipher the four-figure code groups of the Chinese code book. Methods vary. A common method is to use the first line of English text. If we use the line already quoted, we have:

> It was dusk when the priest came.
> 26 804 1753 9

Here 0 is placed below A, the first letter of the alphabet; 1 under D, the second letter in this alphabetic sequence; 2 under I, the third letter in this alphabetic sequence; 3 under K; 4 and 5 under S, which is repeated; and so on.

This rearrangement of the ten numerals to make a figure-enciphering table is placed under the normal order:

```
0 1 2 3 4 5 6 7 8 9
2 6 8 0 4 1 7 5 3 9
```

According to this table, a four-figure group like 3682 would become 0738; that is, 3 becomes 0, 6 becomes 7, 8 becomes 3, and 2 becomes 8.

While I was mulling this over, it occurred to me that the decipherment of the first five-letter groups of the whole series of messages at the office might disclose other words besides *her, light, grain* or *groin,* and that the words themselves might reveal the type of English book used as a key.

The music in the other room had long since been turned off, as had the lights. Schwer must be asleep, or so I surmised. I woke up one of the servants, who led me downstairs to the ground floor with a flashlight and unlocked the chain to the steel gate that protects the compound against thieves.

At the office I worked the rest of the night, and though many English words emerged, none gave me a clue to the nature of the book, except that in one case I deciphered the words *he said,* possibly, though not certainly, indicating a fictional source.

3

The identification of the book in use seemed a hopeless task, until I saw Fidelity. I knew I could trust her, and I was satisfied that she served the Hatchet Man. Now, on our way to dinner with the One-Armed Bandit, I prompted her again.

"You still remember the words?" I asked.

"I think so." She smiled. "Her, light, grain or groin."

"Good. They'll be on consecutive pages, the first word of each page, I think; possibly among the first one hundred pages."

"I remember."

We were at the Bandit's chateau. I took her arm as she stepped from the car. "Nervous?"

"A little."

"Now don't take any chances," I cautioned. "His study is off a guest room ladies usually use. If there's not enough time to look through his English books, simply jot down the titles."

"I'll manage somehow," she said.

The house that the One-Armed Bandit occupied was a detached chateau built of stones quarried from a temple ruin. It was of two stories and spacious. It was not, however, elaborately furnished. The few articles of furniture were for use, and the whole place had an air of transitoriness not uncharacteristic of a much-bombed city. But in this case I suspected that our host was ready to leave at a moment's notice and cared nothing for what he left behind him.

The Bandit was clad in white cotton trousers, silk shirt, and colored flowing tie, the empty sleeve folded and secured with a gold jeweled pin. When his servant led us to him, he smiled engagingly and revealed his fine white teeth. He was a handsome, lively fellow in his thirties, slender and of wiry build, a sardonic gleam in his dark eyes. He must have enjoyed my surprise when he presented his companion, undoubtedly a white woman, fair and very beautiful.

Fidelity, who was carrying a light cape, vanished into the guest room to deposit it but returned almost immediately. It would not do to arouse the shadow of a suspicion at this time.

The beautiful blonde's name proved to be Dorothy, but nothing of her origins or of her connections, except what so obviously appeared to be her relation to the Bandit, came out in the small talk before dinner. I gathered that she had been around, but she did not appear especially intelligent, and if she was engaged in espionage, her employers were probably getting very little for their money. Nor did the Bandit seem infatuated with her. She was for show, to impress the visiting white man with the Bandit's prowess. At that, he was a handsome devil, and I'd not have blamed Dorothy for being in love with him.

We drank several brandies before dinner.

"Success to each in his own business," said the Bandit, *kampeiing* me.

I acknowledged the toast, wondering if this was a warning to mind my own affairs. What he knew of me I did not know, but probably too much. He would have been greatly surprised to know what I had learned of him — surprised and perhaps disturbed.

"You have enjoyed your visit?" he asked.

This was sheer mockery, for no one in his right mind could enjoy much-bombed Chungking.

"Very much," I said. "But I shall enjoy more returning to my own country, as is natural."

"I hope," said the Bandit, challenging me to another drink, "that in that case your return may be soon."

"Very shortly," I said. "I hope to wind up my affairs within a few weeks at most — perhaps in a few days."

How much he believed of this I couldn't know, but it did no harm to create as much doubt as possible in his mind. Even though he had learned of my Black Chamber work, he could not be sure that it was not cover for something else. The very fact that such seemed my job made it suspect. It could be that I was selling munitions or floating a loan in Chinese bonds while pretending to be engaged solely in codes and ciphers.

And Fidelity. Where did she fit in? Did he guess as much as I did of her calling and connections? He was probably in a position to know more, having sources of information denied me. But this again was not sure. Fidelity, drinking sherry, where the Bandit and I drank brandy, betrayed nothing. She was too cool a hand to be indiscreet.

Nothing came out during the dinner, which was elaborate and long, with all manner of dishes strange to me and of what ingredients God knows. I did not ask, and the innumerable cups of hot yellow wine kept me from caring much.

We had no more than finished dinner when the siren blew. The Bandit apologized, withdrew briefly, and returned, dressed in his uniform. If the planes bombed Chungking, as was almost sure to be the case, the opportunity for which I had coached

Fidelity would come. We were in luck, if anything contingent on a bombing raid can be considered lucky.

"We'll have time for some drinks," said the Bandit, whose capacity seemed endless.

Servants brought champagne properly iced, and all of us drank. The Bandit gave us directions to his dugout should the planes come our way. We had another drink, and the Bandit went off to his official duties. I wished he would take Dorothy with him and leave us the run of the place, but he did not suggest it.

The emergency shrieked suddenly, a sound that shatters the nerves, however often it is heard. The fans fluttered to a stop and the lights dimmed to dark, glowing threads and expired. A servant brought candles, which he placed so that they could not be seen from outside. We sat on the rear screened veranda, overlooking the garden that ran to the edge of the Little River. The lights across the river faded, all but one. We heard shots, and it, too, disappeared. Chinese combat planes roared overhead, the sound easily distinguishable from the deeper voice of the Japanese bombers.

Fidelity finished her glass of wine, cast me a look, and drawing a small pencil flashlight from her purse, switched it on and excused herself. It was clearly my job to engross Dorothy's attention and keep her from following Fidelity. Dorothy was too fearful of the impending raid to respond as an attractive woman should to polite advances. I endeavored to question her about her experiences in Hong Kong. She replied distractedly. There was the sound of planes overhead. Dorothy rose, trembling.

"Those are Chinese planes," I said reassuringly and lighted her a cigarette. "Planes make you nervous?" I asked, certainly an asinine remark, for Dorothy was quivering like a colt.

"I'm not used to them," she said.

Clearly she had not been much in Chungking if that was so. I wondered where the Bandit had found her that she should come all the way from Hong Kong to see him. She volunteered nothing. If not intelligent, she was certainly discreet.

"The planes you hear are Chinese planes," I said again. "While you hear those, there is nothing to worry about. When the Japanese planes appear, the Chinese will vanish."

She cocked an ear. Unmistakably, the sound of Chinese planes was growing faint.

"They're leaving now!" cried Dorothy in a panic, and started again to her feet.

"Just making a wide circle," I said with more confidence than I felt. What the devil could Fidelity be doing, anyhow — making an inventory of the house?

"A little wine will steady your nerves," I said and poured a glass with so shaky a hand that I spilled a few drops on her dress.

Dorothy took one sip and rose again determinedly. It was clear that no further blandishments would prevail.

"I'll call Fidelity," I said brightly, and stepped in front of Dorothy to precede her from the room. I wanted to call out a warning, but that wouldn't do. I awkwardly brushed against the table and knocked over a small ornament. The noise it made was inconsequential. I thought of stumbling and falling on my face, but was spared this final ignominy. In the dimness I saw Fidelity approaching. I peered anxiously into her face and she nodded slightly. She looked worn and apprehensive.

From overhead came again the sound of planes, obviously Japanese this time. One of the things I wanted least was to enter that dugout, but politeness demanded that I accompany the women there. I loathe and abhor caves and dread suffocation in them. Green with fright, I went with them. Dorothy was nervous; Fidelity silent and pensive. I was too scared to talk and waited out the raid in tortured silence. The cave shook with the explosions, whose sound was muffled and remote. With each vibration a slight rush of air shook the flames of the wax candles. At long last the sounds and the vibrations ceased.

"It's all over," I said, eager to get out, but I had difficulty in persuading Dorothy that the danger was past. However, the all-clear soon sounded, and the fans and lights came on. I looked anxiously at Fidelity. It seemed to me that her dark skin showed a tinge of pallor, but I dismissed the thought as the product of my apprehensions.

"I must go," she said to Dorothy in a taut voice. "Please thank our host for me."

The situation was awkward for me. Properly, I should have remained with Dorothy until the Bandit's return, but Fidelity's tone was insistent.

Dorothy happily said the right thing. "I'll be all right," she said. "Run along."

"I live across the river," Fidelity explained further.

Outside the dugout she seized my arm and said in a low voice, "Let's get out of here, quick!"

I started the car and soon we were on the Chengtu Road, already crowded with returning traffic — cars, trucks, rickshas, pedestrians enveloped in a choking cloud of dust. All Chung-king was returning to its anthill.

"Now tell me what happened," I said.

"The book is Pearl Buck's *Good Earth*," she said. "I found the three words you gave me on pages seventeen, eighteen, and nineteen."

"That's marvelous!" I said. "You're a brave girl. You had trouble, though. Serious?"

She said slowly, "I'm afraid so. There were several English books in his bookcase, a volume of English plays, Shakespeare, Milton, *The Three Principles,* and half a dozen others, including *The Good Earth.*" She paused.

"But what happened?" I said, my first elation touched with the cold finger of fear.

"I tried some of the other books. I knew I was taking a long time, but I wanted to be thorough and I knew you would keep Dorothy occupied. I saw no servants, and I was sure they were in the dugout. So I kept looking and finally found what you wanted. Then, as I was carefully returning *The Good Earth* to the bookcase, I thought I heard a footstep. I turned off my flash, went into the bedroom, and softly closed the door. Everything was in darkness, but I felt someone was there — a servant perhaps. I kept on walking. I could see the candle light outside. Then I ran into you."

I thought, but did not say, This is very bad.

"You think that whoever was there knows you came from the study?"

"I think so. Stop at the next corner. I'll stay with my friends tonight."

"The gambler's wife?"

"Yes. I knew her in Shanghai. You can trust her." I started to get out to go with her. "No," she said. "Just let me out and drive on."

"You're leaving tomorrow night," I said. "I want to see you before you go."

"Come after dark then. Go to the poolroom. Then follow my friend."

I drove away as she had directed, but with misgivings. Until she was safely out of Chungking, I'd be uneasy. But brooding would not help, and there was work to be done as quickly as possible.

At the office I found Wu and Ling ready to turn in, together with a sullen chauffeur, who resented my running off with the car. Wu addressed vacancy: "It is said in the Ancient Wisdom that a bald head is more likely to acquire a fresh young woman than wisdom."

"None of your wisecracks," I admonished him. "We have work to do. Have either of you boys read *The Good Earth*?"

They said that they had, and I demanded which of them had a copy. Chinese-like, they shook their heads.

"Isn't there a public library here?"

They declared they had never heard of one.

"Where did you read it, then?"

"In Hawaii," said Wu.

"And you, Ling?"

"I forget. I think it was in Hankow."

"In Hankow? Whose copy did you read? You hadn't enough money to buy a copy."

"I might have had," Ling said sadly. "Gold wasn't always eighteen to one. Once it was two to one."

"Even that would have been seven Chinese bucks," I reminded him. "Where did you borrow it?"

"From a priest, perhaps."

"You're not sure?"

"No. Maybe I borrowed it from the university. I did some work there."

"That's better. Now where are the closest universities?"

"There are three up north — what's left of them. They've been retreating with the government for two years."

"How far up north?" The problem of finding a copy of *The Good Earth* was becoming absurdly difficult.

"Maybe sixty *li.*"

"And a *li* is what?"

"Three *li* one mile."

Wu said, "You're excited, Adviser. You know Chinese saying: 'To wise man need for woman not so great tomorrow morning.'"

"This is not a woman," I said, "and we have a saying that a wise man does not leave to tomorrow what must be done today. Wu, have the chauffeur fill up the tank. There should be some gas left in the drum. And Ling, round up the ten students I teach English to."

These were the best of the lot. They spoke a few words of English, and were friendly to me because I spent some time with them trying to teach them the sound of *th*. They had listed every English word with *th* in it. Once I had taught them how to hold the tongue, they made fine progress. In turn, they had taught me how to hold my tongue when saying *shih* in Chinese — a sound that requires one to spit like a cat and hiss like a snake simultaneously.

When the boys showed up, sleepy-eyed, I told them we were working all night and that if we were successful, I'd see that they got a raise.

"We're going to work on the Bandit's messages," I told them. "I have some ideas. We have nearly one hundred intercepts. Divide them among you. Rewrite them, leaving plenty of space between code words, enough for Chinese decipherment and an English translation."

Adjoining my office is a large room with long tables and stools. They went to the files, got the batch of telegrams, and distributed them among themselves.

"How many copies of the Chinese telegraph code book have we?" I asked.

"Only four, Adviser," said Chu, the smartest.

"We need six more, one for each of you. Where can we get them?"

"At the telegraph office, perhaps," said Chu. "Or at headquarters."

"Okay. I appoint you and Wu a committee of two to dig up six more copies. It's late, but dig them up somehow. Ling and I will be back soon."

In the car I said to Ling, "I want to get there as soon as possible, but let's not break a spring on these roads." Though we hit bottom all the way, miraculously the springs held.

Our first stop was at a series of long bamboo and mud huts and dormitories. Ling knew one of the professors, who taught, of all things in a nation at war, political economy. He was an obliging soul and, taking my flashlight, led us through winding cinder paths to a hut door, which he unlocked with a long and ancient Chinese key. Then he proudly showed us his collection of some fifty books in English. Among them, as he had said, was *The Good Earth.*

"You must be starved for English reading, Mr. Osborn," he observed politely. "Maybe you would like *The Three Principles* also. It is a fine translation of our patriot's lectures."

"At another time, when I am free to give it the attention it deserves, I should be delighted to read it," I said, endeavoring to hide my impatience. "But now I have little leisure. *The Good Earth* I have already read, but I wish to reread it while I am in China."

"You have met Dr. Buck, of course?"

"Dr. Buck?" I asked blankly. "Who is he?"

"An honored foreigner, our most respected. He really understands China." He shook his head sadly. "He is also Pearl Buck's ex-husband."

"But he does not write. Is that it?" I asked.

He shrugged and smiled.

At the office I found most of the boys asleep on the floor and on the tables, their work done. They rubbed their eyes when I came in and bent over me as I began to figure out encipherment tables from *The Good Earth*.

"What makes you think the keys are in *The Good Earth?*" Ling asked.

"A little bird told me. The same little bird told me some months ago that Wang Ching-wei was deserting."

Ling nodded. "Birds," he remarked, "are very observant. Also, some are very pretty."

4

The system of the One-Armed Bandit's cipher proved to be simple — provided one had the key. To the number of the month plus the day of the month, ten had been added. Thus, the key for April 1, I found on page 15: 4 + 1 + 10. All the numeral keys were based on the same system.

As I worked these out, Ling made a number of copies and passed them around so that not a moment was lost. Wu and Chu returned with additional copies of the Chinese telegraph code book, and each student now had a copy. With Wu acting as messenger boy and seeing to it that everyone was supplied with work, and Chu acting as supervisor, aiding any student who got stuck, the decipherment of almost one hundred messages progressed rapidly.

As time wore on and the meanings unfolded, I heard exclamations of surprise in half a dozen dialects. Despite my desire to hurry on with the work, I stopped to learn the reason. What we had discovered surpassed anything we had accomplished hitherto. The One-Armed Bandit was the Chungking mouthpiece of Wang Ching-wei, reporting daily through undercover correspondents in Shanghai.

"The dirty double-crosser!" I heard Wu suddenly exclaim. "And I knew him in Berlin, too."

"Now what?" I asked.

"Our German antiaircraft adviser, Herr Wiener. Here's a message directing Japanese bombers to come in at twelve thousand feet. Chinese guns will be timed to burst at least a thousand feet lower."

"Well," I said mildly, "you're hardly surprised at that, are you? Chinese flak never hit anything yet."

"The Hatchet Man will take care of Herr Wiener," Wu said with venom.

I doubted that. I pointed out that he was a German officer and that Hitler intimidated everyone, even as far away as China. Wu laughed.

"He won't be publicly executed," he said, "but something will happen to him. He will be taken suddenly sick, perhaps. Would the Adviser like to make a small bet that Herr Wiener will be alive forty-eight hours from now?"

The Adviser was not willing to put money on it. Much less would he wager on the One-Armed Bandit's survival, as message after message revealed his traffic with the traitor Wang Ching-wei — messages bidding for peace at any price, messages revealing sabotage, bribery, and even incipient plans for a *coup d'état*. Many Chinese were named. I was proud that but one white man was shown to be a traitor, and he a Nazi German.

The sun had risen by the time the last message was deciphered. I gathered all my helpers together.

"Don't leave for a moment, boys," I said and called Wu and Ling into the next room.

"We've got a problem," I told them. "Ten students and we three know more than is healthy for anyone to know. If this information leaks out, one of us will be accused. For myself, I'd not like that at all. I'm too far from home."

Wu and Ling looked grave as the import of my words came to them.

"What should we do?" Ling asked.

"I think," I replied, "that we should go in a group to Number One and consider ourselves under self-imposed house arrest until he has rounded up all the traitors."

"I'm already jittery," said Wu, and Ling nodded agreement.

"Get the chauffeur's keys, then," I told Wu. "I'll drive us all to the Hatchet Man's."

"You think I don't know you have a key?" Wu asked impudently but nevertheless obeyed.

5

We gathered in the Hatchet Man's reception room, and Wu sent a servant to beard the lion in his den and say the Adviser had sensational information that could be conveyed only in person. I had stationed Ling in the outer room to shoo away the servants.

The Hatchet Man, with sleep still in his eyes, was polite but inwardly angry, I could see, at being so rudely awakened. But his anger turned quickly to fierceness as Wu talked with him. At last, when Wu had finished and showed him some of the messages, a smile softened his features, and he shook hands with each of us, giving, I gathered, a word of praise. To me, he was graciousness itself.

"Did you tell the general we wish to confine ourselves to his quarters?" I asked Wu.

"The general says we are all trusted but nevertheless thinks your suggestion a wise one."

"Please tell him also that the Adviser does not wish to lose face, and he has promised rewards to everyone."

"The general says each will be rewarded. And that includes you also."

"Tell the general," I said, "that I'll settle for a drink, breakfast, and bed."

The general smiled broadly at that, clapped his hands, and gave his servants peremptory orders. Then he spoke to Wu.

"The general asks to be excused. He must go to headquarters immediately."

The Hatchet Man bowed and left quickly, the messages clutched in his fist. Watching his long strides, I thought, There'll be hell in Chungking today.

I slept in my old room, far into the afternoon. When I got up, I found Wu and Ling giddy as goats over a bottle of the Hatchet Man's best Scotch.

"Where's everyone?" I asked.

"All gone," Wu said thickly. "A messenger came from Number One an hour ago, saying we need stay no longer."

"Then all the traitors have been rounded up."

"I told you," Wu said, grinning drunkenly, "that Herr Wiener would never see another sunrise, or sunset either."

"And the One-Armed Bandit?"

Wu drew a forefinger expressively across his throat and tried at the same time to swallow his drink.

"No more whiskey, no more girls," said Wu and all but wept at the thought.

"You guys are drunk," I said severely. "How much did Number One give you?"

"We don't know yet," said Wu, "but enough, we hope, to buy a concubine."

"How much is that?"

"Five thousand for one with fine feathers," Wu replied. "Six hundred for a used model. But as you say, it's not the initial cost but the upkeep."

I left them dreaming of concubines and drove to Schwer's. He wasn't in. I changed clothes, had a bite to eat, and at sundown walked to the poolroom, where I found Marguerite waiting. She said no word, but giving me a scarcely perceptible nod, walked down the street. I followed her down a twisting alleyway almost to the Yangtze's edge, dodging rats as best I could. She turned in at a court and mounted wooden steps to a suite of rooms on the second floor. There, she disappeared without a word, and I was left alone with Fidelity, who looked as cool as ever. As for me, despite my loss in weight, I still sweated in streams.

"You look pleased with yourself," she said, smiling, and lighted cigarettes.

"The credit is all yours," I said, and meant it. Then, after a moment's silence, I remarked tentatively, "Fidelity, you never talk about yourself — "

"Neither do you talk about yourself," she interrupted me.

"It is safer so," I agreed. "But I'm worried about your safety, and you don't help any by your silence."

"What is it you want to know?" she asked. "Perhaps I can help you."

"Just this. Why don't you go to the general — you know the one I mean — and ask for protection? Or at least release me from our unspoken bond of secrecy. The Bandit's servant or someone saw you in his study. Doubtless the Bandit knew why you were there. From his many connections he almost certainly knew what I'm doing in China. Thanks to you, the Bandit has been taken and is probably dead by this time. But his servant or some follower may still be at large and looking for you. Let me go to the general and ask for protection."

She would not hear of it.

"Then go yourself," I urged, "before it's too late. Let me take you."

"No, that isn't necessary. No one but you and my two friends know where I am. I'm leaving for the airport tonight. My baggage I am leaving at the South Springs and taking nothing but my papers."

"Your name is on the passenger list?"

"Another name; not mine, certainly. Let's talk of something else."

At ten, Marguerite returned. "It's time to go," she said.

Fidelity gave me a Hong Kong address through which she could be reached.

"I'll go along with you," I said.

She would not permit that, saying that, as a foreigner, I would be too conspicuous. She would go alone. I was still apprehensive. When she had left, I turned to Marguerite. "You think she's all right?"

"Of course," Marguerite assured me.

I hunted out Schwer a second time and found him tearfully drinking my imported gin.

"Where's the girl friend?" I asked him.

"She ran away," he said.

"Anything else missing?"

"Just my three hundred investment."

We were poor company for each other, and after a few drinks I walked to the poolroom. None of my friends was around, and I was about to leave after watching a game of billiards when I saw Marguerite enter by the back way. Her face was pale beneath the rouge on her yellow cheeks.

"She didn't get away," she said in a low voice.

"What!" I exclaimed. "Where is she?"

"Drowned on her way to the airport. Someone overturned her sampan."

My worst fears had been realized, and there was nothing I could do. I turned away without a word.

· Chungking, August 1939

I AM STILL LIVING WITH SCHWER while scouring the city for a place of my own. The Service wants me to move to safety, as they call it, across the river beyond the Second Range, but life is sufficiently barren even in the city. Here I may die a violent death, but in the country I should certainly die of boredom. My students urge me to become a country squire and landowner. Foreigners may not own land here, but many do through the subterfuge of buying property and getting a friendly Chinese to be listed as owner.

Hearing me one day complain of settling an old financial debt in America, Ling said, "Adviser, stay in China. Here you are rich. At Shanghai black market rates you make twenty thousand Chinese dollars each month. With that you can buy a farm. In one year you will be a rich landowner, with many hundred Chinese acres."

"So what?"

"Also many concubines" — at which he wet his lips.

"But I don't want to die in China."

"You are indeed hard to please," said Ling sadly.

I did not remind him that my contract is nearly up and that I am seriously thinking of returning to the United States. Obviously I am not cut out for life in the Orient. It becomes more difficult for me day by day. The filth, disease, misery, and poverty are unbearable, and I find fewer excuses for them in China's desperate plight and the existing state of war. I cannot become like Schwer and the Chinese themselves, so inured to these conditions that I shut my eyes to them. There is, indeed, much talk of reforms, but from my observation of the Chinese, Ling's quotation of an old Chinese saying is wholly apt:

> Chinese meet.
> They confer.
> They discuss.
> They decide.
> They do nothing.

It is also true, unfortunately, that those who do most of the talking have no sympathy for the coolie class, who do all the fighting and bear most of the miseries. These are considered a race apart and are treated as our Negroes are treated in the South. Agrarian reform does not mean that peasant sharecroppers reduced to the starvation level are to receive any larger share of the crops, nor does postwar voting include the right of coolies to vote. The Kuomintang, whose members are hand-picked, like the members of the Kelly and Hague machines, and who talk loosely of postwar economic and political reforms, has no more intention of turning government over to coolies than have our Southern states of turning government over to the Negroes.

"Poverty and disease I understand," I once said to Schwer. "But why filth? Why, just because you're poor, must you have a pool of excrement at your front doorstep? Why sleep with pigs and chickens?"

He was damned if he knew, but remarked that unless America had changed greatly since he was last home, there was plenty of filth wherever there was poverty and disease.

At tiffin now and then at Pop Neilson's compound along the Little River I hear much talk of what China is to be after "final victory" — a favorite Chinese expression, though to the best of my knowledge they have yet to win *any* victory. Pop, though a Dane, claims German citizenship, since there is no Danish government representative here to protect him. He's about seventy-five, sports a kaiser mustache together with a Vandyke, and has lived in Chungking for forty-five years. Formerly he made munitions for whatever warlord was in power, but is now reduced to the status of expert blacksmith — when he is sober, which I gather isn't often. He has for some time promised to make me a coffee roaster and an ice cream freezer, but I've not got them yet. His compound, two stories high, with a typical tiled roof, is built of brick and bamboo. Workshop and storage space take the ground floor, and on the second are a number of bedrooms, a Chinese kitchen, servants' quarters, and a large dining room, where he serves tiffin to a nondescript lot of Chinese and foreigners.

The servants make a good thing out of trafficking in girls for English and American sailors from the small gunboats lying at anchor here, and Pop himself receives the price of the rooms. The sailors are brazen in their love affairs, but now and then I see a foreign diplomat sneaking down the back stairs when he thinks the coast is clear, hoping thus to be unseen, lest he lose face in diplomatic society here, such as it is.

I eat only occasionally at Pop's, for whenever I do, I get into an argument with the Chinese about something or other. My latest quarrel was with a Chinese doctor, who said, "After we win the final victory we will industrialize China."

"We?" I said. "Who in hell is we?"

The Chinese doctor, trained in Japan, spoke fair English. There were present, also, a Chinese dentist, a Chinese colonel, a Chinese merchant, a Greek importer, Schwer, and Pop.

"We?" the doctor exclaimed angrily. "I mean all of us."

"Would you include Chinese doctors?" I asked nastily. "Did you yourself ever bind a soldier's wound?"

"I haven't been to the front," he said and flushed.

"Listen, Bud," I said. "Chungking is the front. Plenty die here. And I happen to know you're one of the many Chinese doctors who ran away after the May bombings. When you say *we* will win the victory, you mean the coolies. You educated Chinese wouldn't fight with the Japanese if they were at the city walls."

I thought the colonel, a big fellow, would punch me in the nose, but instead all four Chinese got up and stamped out angrily, gesticulating and talking excitedly.

"I'm sorry, Pop," I said.

"Ach," he replied, "to hell mit 'em."

To show his appreciation he opened a bottle of imported brandy and poured us each a drink.

"*Erste heute,*" he said, a strictly Chungking toast. Then, hearing conversation in the adjoining bedroom, he hid the bottle. "Dos damn sailors." He grinned, showing two yellow teeth.

The sailor, a big handsome blond youngster, came in with a pretty Chinese girl, no more than thirteen, I judged. He sat at the table, the girl on his lap. "How about a drink, Pop?" he said.

"No drinks today. Tomorrow maybe."

The sailor playfully pinched the girl's ear. "Tell him."

The little girl looked up innocently at Pop and said, "Go to hell, you sonofabitch."

Pop laughed and unbent sufficiently to pull out the bottle and pour each a glass.

"That's better," the sailor said. "I'm going back tomorrow. My time's up."

"What will you do at home for yellow girls?" I asked. "You'll miss them."

"I'd swap this slope-head for a white one right now."

To my knowledge, only American sailors call Chinese "slope-heads."

I had seen him before with the same little girl. She lived across the Little River but somehow learned of his presence at Pop's so quickly that he had time for not more than two drinks before she appeared, grinning happily. She was happy no doubt because his generosity would appease her *amah's* wrath. He was good to her and paid her handsomely. What the division of spoils was between her and Pop's servants, I do not know, but on her return to her *amah* owner she would, according to Chinese custom, be stripped and searched, and if she tried to hold back so much as a few pennies, would be severely beaten. At some future time, when her usefulness as a prostitute neared the end, she would be released by her owner and would in turn purchase a young girl from some impoverished coolie mother and rear the child to prostitution as security against old age. In China, even in the vice racket, there is no old age or unemployment problem.

The Greek's compound is close to Pop's. As the sailor and his girl were leaving, the Greek's three children, aged five to eight, clambered up the stairs, calling to him in Chinese. His children all look Chinese. Ling swears the Greek is not the father — probably the Chinese cook, Ling says. But he is prejudiced, disliking to believe that any Chinese woman, however low her station in life, would prefer a foreigner. He feels shame for his race even when Chinese prostitutes sleep with foreigners.

"What do they say?" I asked the Greek.

"They want to play with the two Russian children," he said.

Pop looked significantly at me.

"They've gone to the country," I said.

But they had not gone to the country. They had been kidnapped and flown to Shanghai. I had not wished to be involved but there are times when one cannot stand idly by and keep one's self-respect. It was the old story of the white woman who marries a Chinese, only to discover later when he brings her back to China that she is not a wife but a servant-concubine.

Zelda, a Russian Jewess, against the advice of the Soviet government had married a wealthy Chinese army officer in Moscow. A few years later the officer was recalled to China, and Zelda, with her two male children by him, came too. The officer's parents, who lived in Chengtu, having no other grandsons, took possession of the boys and refused to permit the mother to direct their education. The officer, shedding his veneer of Western culture, took a new concubine and degraded his Russian wife to the status of a servant. Then the grandparents pulled wires to secure a legal divorce and the custody of the children.

Desperate, Zelda flew to Chungking to consult with her Russian friend, Stephanie, proprietress of a small restaurant. I had seen Zelda about town but knew nothing of her plight until about ten days ago, when Stephanie beckoned me to a back room off her restaurant and showed me two sleeping children, aged, I guessed, two and three years. They were beautiful children, with yellow hair but with the low-bridged nose indicative of Chinese blood.

"Yours?" I asked.

"No," she said, and was relating the story when Zelda entered. She had flown to Chengtu and, by bribing the servants, had kidnapped her two children and flown back to Chungking with them.

"You'll never get away with this," I said.

"You can help us," Zelda said eagerly.

I looked at her closely. She was not over twenty-five but was worn and haggard. So, I thought, this is why you've been selling yourself both to foreigners and Chinese. Airplane tickets are expensive.

"You know the CNAC manager," Zelda said. "He will sell Stephanie a seat to Hong Kong if you ask him to. You don't have to book the children. Stephanie can take them on her lap."

"But the children are yours."

"Yes, but I can't get a release — not quickly. I'm doing work for the Chinese government. They won't let me go. But I've got to get the children away quickly. My husband will be looking for them."

Another secret agent, I guessed.

"Why don't you go to the Russian embassy for protection?" I asked.

"I lost my Russian citizenship when I married. I was told in

Moscow that if I must marry a Chinese, marry one on the east coast, one with Russian citizenship. Instead, I married this dog."

I promised to go at once to the CNAC office, and advised the women to hide the children elsewhere after dark.

"You know Pop, don't you? He'll hide them for you."

They had taken my advice, and the Greek's children had seen them at breakfast the next morning. But Stephanie had got away with them before discovery, and a few days later a message came, telling of their safe arrival in Shanghai.

Zelda was elated and sought me out to tell me the good news.

"My husband is here. I must get away before he has me arrested."

"I wouldn't try it," I warned her.

"But I must. You'll help me to get a seat to Hong Kong? I want to go tomorrow night."

I had arranged for that and now at Pop's I felt very smug about the whole matter. When the Greek and his children had gone, Schwer said, "Did you hear about Zelda?"

"Sure. I told you I helped her."

"Well, you didn't help much. At the airport she was refused passage and threatened with arrest."

"I warned her of that."

"That isn't the end. She became hysterical and on the way to shore jumped into the river. You know what that means."

"Yes," I said, remembering Fidelity. "I know what that means."

· *Chungking, September 1939*

*R*ECENTLY I ASSUMED A NEW ROLE, in addition to my other and sufficient duties. I was asked to give an oral English examination to a group of young Chinese college graduates, both male and female. Chinese linguists from headquarters were to examine them in French, German, Russian, and Japanese, and those who passed were to receive courses in espionage and counterespionage. I learned to my disgust that I was to be one of the instructors in these courses.

Over half of the applicants had selected English as their entrance test. At headquarters they were brought one at a time before Ling, Wu, and me. Ling kept tab of their names, and I gave the grades on the understanding and speaking of English. I was generous in the grading, for even Americans are sometimes put to it to understand my Hoosier drawl, and I charitably passed twenty. I would have failed the lot had I realized that not only was I to lecture to them two hours each week, through interpreters, on espionage and counterespionage, but was also to spend another two hours teaching my group English.

I tried to evade the task at our first English gathering by dividing the class into two debating teams. The debates were to be extemporaneous, and as each student spoke I planned to keep notes of his errors in grammar and pronunciation — of such, that is, as my meager education enabled me to recognize. Most Chinese try to follow the pronunciation accepted in England, so, in order not to lose face, I had a dictionary handy in which to look up disputed words before getting out on a limb. As for grammatical errors, I was able to recognize a few common ones and quickly built up a reputation as an English professor by pointing out such errors as "he had went" and "I done it." I was popular also because I came to classes late and dismissed them early.

When I had chosen my teams I wrote on the blackboard the subject of our first debate: "Resolved, that the Powers should give up extrality rights in China."

Nowhere in the Far East did I ever hear the word "extraterritoriality," which was lucky for me, because I could never pronounce it.

There was a buzz of protest in Chinese.

"What's the matter?" I asked Ling.

"They ask who takes the negative side."

"Group B. The names are on the blackboard."

The leader of Group B stood up. "Adviser," he said, "my team cannot take the negative side. There is nothing to debate. Every Chinese knows extrality rights were forced on Chinese at the point of a gun."

"In a debate," I pointed out to him, "you don't have to believe in what you say."

Ling, with a sly look, said something in Chinese at which they all laughed and said, *"Shih, shih."*

"Now what?" I asked, but Ling only smiled, and the leader of Group B stood up again. "Adviser," he said, "Mr. Ling has suggested that we all take the affirmative and you the negative."

"That," I said severely, "is an attempt to get out of work. It is you who must do the speaking while I do the correcting."

I ran over in my mind other controversial subjects, but there were objections of one sort or another to all I could think of. Although a Chinese in Chungking is free to say pretty much what he likes, I realized that these students were destined for the Central Government and that, whatever their beliefs, they might hesitate to express them in a classroom. I wasn't qualified to teach English in any accepted sense, and besides, I wanted to learn a little of what young China was thinking. So I decided to take them in turn and question them. The action of the Communist troops and guerrillas under Mao Tse-tung had puzzled me. Perhaps these students could throw some light on the subject, for a number of them had escaped from occupied provinces, working their way to Chungking through points held by Central and Communist troops.

Shortly after my arrival at Chungking I had asked for battle maps and the designation of a man from headquarters to keep them up to date with colored pins. The request had been granted, as was my request for a daily report of the disposition of Japanese and Chinese troops and a bulletin of their encounters. This is the minimum background necessary to any cipher bureau during war.

Recently these reports had shown clashes and even severe battles between Communist and Central troops. Each side seemed more hostile to the other than to the Japanese. In many provinces of occupied China — Shansi, Hopei, Shangtung, Kiangsu, Anhwei — fratricide was the order of the day. There was trouble even in unoccupied Shensi. If one excludes Manchuria or Manchukuo, these states are the northern and northeastern provinces of China. To the northeast of them lies Manchuria, seized by the Japanese in 1931, and farther to the north are Inner and Outer Mongolia.

As a professional cryptographer I had, of necessity, been interested in both Japan and China and had followed Chinese history rather closely, though not with much understanding. I knew vaguely of the overthrow of the Manchus in 1911 by the followers of Sun Yat-sen; of the struggle between warlords, peasants, landowners, and industrialists (yet all alike fighting against foreign imperialism) up to 1928, when most forces joined a coalition under the Kuomintang led by Chiang Kai-shek, who had inherited the leadership on the death of Sun Yat-sen in 1926. Everyone has read of the savage civil war that followed when a small group of extremists or Communists below the Yangtze, composed largely of armed workers and peasants, refused to join the coalition government.

Troops of the Kuomintang set out to annihilate the Communists before they had time to strengthen themselves. The Communists, to acquire followers, killed more and more landlords and gave the land to the peasants. Both sides were as vicious as were the Japanese at Nanking in the present war. Murder, rape, torture, and the burning of villages was the order of the day. Mao Tse-tung, the present Communist leader, with headquarters at Yenan, was in control. In 1934, after years of bitter civil war, seeing that his position south of the Yangtze was untenable, he began the famous march west to Tibet, then to North Shensi, just west of the Yellow River, a distance of fifteen hundred miles. Here, following his former method of land expropriation, he acquired a formidable force and defied the Kuomintang troops, which had harassed him savagely during his northern retreat.

Subsequently the troops of both sides began to fraternize, and late in 1936 Chiang Kai-shek, on a visit to the front to restore order among his disaffected troops, was captured. This started a clamor throughout China for his release. In this, even the Communists joined, for they feared that his death would infuriate the people and lead to popular uprisings against the Communists. Fortunately for China, he was released.

Then, in July 1937, Japan, fearing the united opposition of the Communists and the Kuomintang, provoked an outbreak of hostilities at the Marco Polo Bridge at Shanghai. With Japan the common enemy, both factions temporarily sank their differences. They withdrew gradually before the Japanese but left guerrilla forces to harass the invaders.

Yet now, in 1939, with the war two years old and apparently a stalemate, Communists and Central forces were again fighting each other behind the Japanese lines, with all their former fierceness and cruelty. My daily reports showed this to be so without the shadow of a doubt. I knew, too, that the Generalissimo had sent troops to block any attempt of Mao Tse-tung in North Shensi to march south and seize the communication center of Sian. No foreign reporters were permitted in this territory. But the Communists had had a good press before this, and many distinguished reporters had told romantic tales of the courage, fighting ability, and magnanimity of Communist guerrilla troops. At all these, Ling had laughed.

"Communist guerrillas!" he sneered. "The Chinese word is 'float and fight.' They float but never fight."

"How about Central guerrillas?" I asked.

He shrugged. "Old Wisdom say, 'Good seed for good grain, spoiled grain to poison vermin.' "

However that may be, and whatever their qualities, good or bad, the Communist and Central guerrillas were fighting now — unfortunately against each other.

Six of my students had escaped through occupied territory to Chungking and had had the opportunity to learn facts at first hand.

"Why are they fighting each other?" I asked.

A boy from Shantung said, "The Communists kill you if you do not believe as they do."

I said, "The Communist propagandists here say that Communism is popular and point out that millions are of their party."

"You either accept it or you die," he said gravely.

"They have elections, we are told. The Kuomintang has none."

"No difference," he said. "Here you don't vote. There you vote as you are told."

"How about their co-operatives?" I asked. "You Chinese brag a lot about the co-operatives here, but I know the workers get starvation prices for their goods, which are sold in the stores for fancy prices. Isn't that pretty cruel exploitation?"

"Same thing. Here merchants make the profits. Up there the

Communist government gets it." He thought a moment. "The program for schooling is better there."

"In what way?"

"More peasants are taught to read and write."

All of the six who had escaped through the lines had something to say. It was clear that if you sympathized with Communism you believed one thing, and that if you were anti-Communist you believed something else. Each declared the other to be the aggressor, and there were the usual tales of cold-blooded murder, rape, torture, burning of houses, seizure of property, and burial alive.

I had never believed the latter possible until one night Ling enlightened me. I had gone alone to a movie, a Chinese-made picture in which the Japanese troops rape the mother and dash out the baby's brains. This picture also depicted the Japanese burying Chinese civilians alive. You don't need to understand the Chinese language to follow a Chinese melodrama.

I saw Ling after the show.

"How did you like it?" he asked.

"I swallowed the rape and the murder," I said, "but not the burying people alive. That's poor propaganda."

A look of amazement crossed his face. "You don't believe they do that?"

"No," I said.

"Well, they do. And so do we. In China it is the custom for the head of the family to punish all others. If a son does bad things and cannot be controlled, he is buried alive."

From my talks with my students, it was apparent that the Red and White terrors, waged from 1928 to 1937 in a civil war of extermination, had broken out again, though on a smaller scale. The men on both sides had the same heritage, the same customs, the same moral standards. A new economic philosophy does not change overnight a man's method of waging war. Both sides must bear alike the charge of barbarity and inhumanity.

Faced with the common enemy, Japan, the civil factions might again consent to bury their differences, but once the war was ended, fratricide would break out anew and would continue until one side had wholly conquered the other. In such a conflict Mao Tse-tung would be a formidable foe to the Kuomintang. He had more than promises to offer the peasants. For the murder of the landlords and their retainers, Mao Tse-tung could give the peasants free land. The Kuomintang gave no more than vague promises of postwar reform. Meanwhile, as taxes grew, the misery of the workers and farm coolies mounted, for their masters passed on the burden of new taxes, whether in money or grain, to the workers and the sharecroppers. Inflation increased with alarming speed, and with each new tax the workers ate less.

Young Chinese in unoccupied territory pretended to be liberal and to follow Marxian ideas after the manner of Sun Yat-sen — or so it seemed to me. They, like the Kuomintang, talked loudly of postwar reforms and the industrialization of China. Mao Tse-tung offered his followers land for the taking. They constituted a fighting minority who would never be conquered but by the sword. Whatever the truces between the rival parties, there could be but one eventual outcome — a renewal of bloody civil war.

2

With Wu and Ling interpreting, I spent two hours each week with the entire group of students, giving them a smattering of codes and ciphers and secret inks. I also called in the sabotage chemists and engineers (still alive, rather to my surprise) for demonstration of incendiary pencils and the like, making sure that my interpreters and I were at a safe distance.

In teaching my class how to evade the censor by sending apparently innocent messages in the Chinese public code book, I nearly got us all into trouble, but with the happy consequence of bringing my lectures to an end. I gave prizes for the best three messages passed by the censor and sent to a fictitious person and address in Hong Kong. Prizes were to be paid only if the messages got through. That they did so we knew when inquiries came back, stating the addressee was unknown. The censor therefore pricked up his ears and, getting wind of a foreigner being mixed up in it, came to see me during a lecture. He brought the originals with him. These showed the texts before encodement but not, of course, the phony secret message.

The first message in Chinese said, "Please tell my cousin to send me airmail two hundred quinine tablets." The so-called secret message, encrypted by a device I showed them, read, "New airfield completed six miles up Little River."

The chief censor, a general, was red with rage and scarcely did me the courtesy to bow.

There was an impish look on Ling's face. "The general wants to know," he translated, or pretended to translate, "what all this monkey business is."

"You're mixed up in this. You tell him."

They went into a long huddle. Ling opened the Chinese code book, took paper and pencil, and jotted down numerals and Chinese characters. The students gathered round, some snickering, while Ling with a straight face made his explanations. At last the general, seemingly mollified, took his leave, first making me an elaborate bow. But he still, I thought, looked a bit uncertain.

"You'll have us all in jail," I said to Ling. "Why did you tell him?"

"I didn't. I told him the secret message read, 'Your firstborn is a male.' That didn't sound so much like a spy's communication."

"But how could you explain such a message. It doesn't say that."

"I can make it say that as easily as anything else," said Ling. "I never did understand the method, anyhow. Neither does the general, but he couldn't admit not understanding. He would lose face."

Whatever the general's state of mind, word quickly came from the Hatchet Man not to tease him anymore, and the lectures, of which I was heartily sick, were discontinued.

3

Late that afternoon I was enjoying a siesta in my room at Schwer's, lying naked on a bamboo mattress with a fan turned on me, when I was rudely shaken. It was Schwer, red-faced and not quite sober.

"Wake up!" he cried. "War in Europe!"

"You're sure?"

"Yes. Hong Kong radio. Germany's invaded Poland, and France and England are declaring war on Germany."

Neither of us believed that America, burned once, would join in again, but we agreed that the situation in China would be altered. Schwer had sold $30,000 Chinese for gold before the news got around. He had paid a little over twenty to one and expected it would be thirty to one within a month. Hitherto, English and American loans had supported Chinese credit. Fearing to offend Japan, England and America might very well do so no longer. China, with her seaports closed and her land occupied, would be in a bad way.

"China'll make peace now," Schwer said.

"I don't think so," I answered halfheartedly.

"Too many want peace," he insisted. "With no imports and only thin lines of exports through Burma and Indo-China, the Chinese businessman can't make money. A few run the blockade, but they mostly trade Chinese paper money back and forth, and the currency drops faster than the profits pile up. Chinese merchants are escaping downriver in a continuous stream. The Japanese are smart enough to encourage them. A Chinese merchant doesn't give a damn who rules him, as long as he can make a profit. We'll have peace soon."

"Not without a *coup d'état,*" I said. "Not so long as the

Generalissimo is alive. He has wealth through the Madame, position, power, and the respect of foreign powers. He's a patriot and wants to make history. He has all to lose and nothing to gain. He'll never give up."

These were brave words, and I almost convinced myself. Yet I felt an uneasy qualm. A quick peace would mean I would have no time to escape. To be captured by the Japanese would be death — a most unpleasant one, doubtless. My new contract had been drawn up and was awaiting my signature. But I had delayed. I could not make up my mind.

To divert my thoughts from these depressing speculations, I asked Schwer if he had ever smoked opium. I had never done so, and it seemed improper to leave Chungking without having been in an opium den. Schwer professed to being an old hand and said it wasn't bad but that "you sort of need a girl."

Opium-smoking is forbidden under China's New Life Movement, along with other vices and manners offensive to Western sensibilities. But inevitably, old ways persist. Four hundred and fifty million Chinese are not to be converted overnight to a wholly different way of life. A good deal of face-saving and hypocrisy is the inevitable accompaniment of the attempt. My teams of students investigating various aspects of Chungking's life in order to report to me in English had had no difficulty in finding opium dens, houses of prostitution, dealers in smuggled goods, and other evidence that China was pursuing the even tenor of her ways as in centuries past. Sun Yat-sen in his *Three Principles of the People* had outlined the New Life Movement, designed to fight superstition, ignorance, and corruption. He was, as Schwer, who had known him, conceded, "a grand old fellow," but the New Life Movement was mostly, in Schwer's opinion, "baloney."

"You remember," said Schwer, "that preacher I introduced you to across the river? Well, he's the guy who directs the New Life Movement for China. The Madame appointed him. Everything is tabu. The missionaries draw up a list a mile long, and the Chinese laugh at it and do as they please. Then the missionaries go back to the States and lecture about the New Life Movement and raise more funds from the suckers. From them you'd think China a paradise." He took a drink. "I should have been a missionary," he said morosely.

Ling had one day expressed the same thought. Pointing to a passing woman missionary, he asked me, "Adviser, how much would she make in America?"

"Oh, I don't know," I said. "A bare subsistence, possibly."

"That one has three servants, a house, and sends her boys to college in America."

"Well," I said, trying to be fair, "I have more than three servants, I have a house, or did have one, and my pay could send my boy to college, too."

"But," he persisted, "did you have a bare subsistence in America?"

"Sometimes less" — I laughed — "sometimes affluence."

Then he had asked, as was usually asked in any discussion of missionaries, "Do you believe in Jesus Christ?"

"Missionaries have been good to you," I told him. "They taught you English at cut rates. They teach you hygiene for nothing. Isn't that enough? What does it matter whether Buddhism or Christianity is the true religion? And besides, don't they feed you rice?"

Said Ling, "It is true, even as Ancient Wisdom says, that beggars cannot be choosers, but in America I imagine none is so poor as to swallow Buddhism with rice."

"Then," I advised, "swallow the rice only and don't go around asking people if they believe in Jesus Christ."

Schwer was curious as to the ways of my students in securing the addresses of opium dens. The leaders of the group had been clever. They roamed the streets until they found an old man who looked like a drug addict. One would approach him and say, "Old man, my venerable mother is ill with pains in her head. Do good deed. Tell me where there are opium ashes and save her from pain. Do good deed. May all your sons have sons and live in peace."

If the old fellow knew, he would tell them where to go to get the ashes, for the Chinese believe, no doubt rightly, that opium ashes are a narcotic. All over town they went and brought back a list of addresses. Other groups brought other lists, and I learned more about Chungking in one week than I'd learned in months. Then my superiors had stopped it. It was not well that a foreigner should learn these things.

Schwer, fearing an air raid, refused to go to an opium den.

"We'd smother on a night like tonight," he said, and indeed sweat was dripping from us and I had broken out in prickly heat. "I'll get you a pipe here, but I'm sticking to Chungking gin."

He clapped his hands and yelled, *"Wei wei."*

Two barefoot houseboys came running. He spoke to them in Szechuan dialect, making signs of smoking and pointing to me.

"Pu shao-ti," they said, shaking their heads.

Schwer picked up an empty gin bottle and they ducked instinctively.

"You still think they spy on you?"

"Of course." He put down the bottle, and the boys stood trembling. "They know damned well what I said. I know they smoke opium. I want them to bring their pipe, but they're afraid."

He took the list of addresses I had given him and spoke to them again, pointing to me and making signs of smoking.

This time they grinned, and when Schwer gave them $20 they bowed, said, *"Ma shan chi,"* and walked slowly away.

"Look at them!" Schwer laughed. *"Ma shan chi* — on horseback go. Always on horseback — and they crawl like snails. I told them to go to your address for a pipe and opium. They'll never part with that twenty bucks."

When they came back it was dark, but they brought with them a paper of opium, a very small oil lamp with a round wick, and a bamboo pipe, the bowl no larger than a marble. Schwer went to his kitchen and brought back a new wick and a bottle of olive oil. Chinese vegetable oil is bad for the lungs, and olive oil for opium smokers is always desirable. He replenished the lamp with olive oil, inserted a new wick, and lit it. Then he filled the pipe with opium and, holding it over the flame, sucked at it until the flame melted the powder so that it could be rolled into a round pill.

"Here you are," he said. "It's simple. Hold the pipe bowl at an angle so that the flame touches the opium and suck on the pipe."

I did as he said and took a few puffs.

"How'm I doing?" I asked.

"Just stretch out and keep at it. But it's no fun without a woman."

I stretched out in the wicker chair, rested my feet on another, and now and then put the flame to the pipe and puffed, waiting patiently for the visions of beautiful dancing girls. Unfortunately, none appeared, but Schwer's face grew dimmer and I became immersed in my own thoughts and, as through a haze, saw the skies clear and the moon rise over the First Range. Then, from some remote chamber of the mind, I heard a wail and woke up, Schwer shaking me.

"Ching pao," he said matter-of-factly.

Again I must have dozed, for he awoke me with the chill application of a wet towel. I got up and watched him draw the bathtub full.

"Always have the bathtub filled in case of fire," he said. "Have a good smoke?"

"Damned if I know," I replied, unable to remember anything. My mouth was dry and sticky. "I'd like a drink of water," I said.

"I told you opium was no good without a woman." He got me a tall glass of cold water, which I drank thirstily.

"Let's get going," he said, and yelled for his servants.

We were at the foot of a long flight of stairs, Schwer a bit tight and I befogged. We waited impatiently. *"Wei wei,"* he yelled. There came the fearful cry of the emergency. Schwer dashed up the stairs, then back again. "The yellow bastards can't find the key!"

Panic seized me and awakened me from my stupor. More than anything I feared being trapped in a building or a dugout.

"Let's get out of here!" I cried.

The iron gate, locked with bolt and chain, barred our way. Schwer led me down the hall. "Here," he said, "hold this," and gave me his flashlight. He threw his heavy body against the office door repeatedly until it gave. Inside, he opened a window and we dropped to the ground. We hurried up the narrow street to the main thoroughfare, where my chauffeur always drove at the first alarm.

"He's beat it," I said, looking vainly around.

"Never mind," said Schwer, "we'll go to a cave," and led the way to the river's edge. Two guards yelled at us, pointing to our clothes, white in the moonlight. "Silly devils," muttered Schwer. "They think the planes can see us."

At the entrance to the dugout Schwer showed his credentials and the guard motioned us in.

"Not me," I said. "I'll sit outside. I'm afraid." I sat down and leaned against the stone entrance. "I'll wait here. I don't like holes in the ground."

Schwer disappeared and the guard preemptorily motioned me down the steps. He started to take hold of me, and I pulled my gun. "*Tso-la,*" I said. He looked at me uncertainly and dropped his hand. I fell asleep.

I was awakened by blasts that knocked me down the steps. My mind now clear, I fought mosquitoes in the darkness until, at last, the all-clear sounded and Schwer emerged amid a stream of humanity. Though fires were burning close by, we were too tired to bother. We waited at his gate until the servants came. Evidently they had found the key. Schwer had none, saying that in China no gentleman ever carries a key, but depends on his servants for all such menial tasks as opening a gate.

On the veranda he turned on the lights and peered at me as

I scratched mosquito bites. Then he produced a bottle. "Try this," he said.

"I don't want a drink," I replied ungraciously.

"It's not a drink. It's ammonia. Good for mosquito bites."

I stripped and rubbed it in, choking on the fumes.

"How about another pipe?" He chuckled, observing my misery. "Opium's good for malaria," he assured me.

Recalling the characteristic Chinese pallor, I was skeptical, and if it was true, the price was too great to pay. The pleasures of opium, like the exotic charms of the East, had in my case proved wholly illusory. Better to enjoy them in the pages of De Quincey than in the flesh, especially if mosquito-bitten.

4

Awakened the next morning by a hailstorm and cold driving rain, I got up to close the windows. Then I went naked onto the veranda and let the rain sprayed through the screens by the high wind soothe my prickly heat and mosquito bites. Schwer came out, rubbing his eyes.

"Look," I said, turning for him to see. "The prickly heat's fading. I told you it would vanish with the first cool weather."

I watched the swirls of rain and hail twisting up and down the Yangtze. A large junk, which was being pulled against the current by coolies lashed to long bamboo ropes, broke away and drifted downstream. Lightning flashed over the First Range, the first I had seen in China. "Just like Indiana," I said.

"You're going home?" Schwer asked.

Comfortable now for the first time in months, I wasn't so sure.

"I may stay," I said, "if I can get the place I've been negotiating for."

It was a small, four-story apartment house close to Schwer's, covered with rubble, the glass gone from the windows and the roof knocked off by bombs.

It was less than half an hour after daylight, but Schwer's

Yardley in Chungking, with two of his students

houseboys were up. They approached and asked, *"Chi fan?"*

"Shih-ti," said Schwer, and seating himself in a wicker chair, put his feet on the porch railing. "It's an easy life here. Why go home?"

Why, indeed, I thought, a question that thousands of white men living at ease in primitive lands must have asked themselves. Why fight the Orient? Why not give in to it? Here lay security, respect, even honor. Yet some faint, protesting voice was not answered.

The servants served breakfast — coffee roasted by Pop's machine and ground, Indian fashion, between stones; Chinese ham; fried soy-bean curd; and a coarse, toasted wheat bread spread with yellow chicken fat in lieu of butter.

"Still too hot for eggs," Schwer said. "They stink by the time the farmers get them in."

"Stink is the most descriptive of all words in China," I said.

"It is," he agreed, "but if you can forget it, as you will in time, China is a fine country for foreigners."

"Foreigners won't always enjoy extrality," I said. "In a few years you'll be hauled into court if you slap your servants."

"Chinese aren't."

"But foreigners will be. And maybe Chinese, too. The Chinese may respect us for our command of modern sciences, but underneath, they hate us. I've seen it too often in their eyes not to know."

"A small matter. The Powers will always force China to recognize our rights."

"And what," I asked, "may they be?"

"Oh, hell. Let's not go into that again. But I'll give you an idea of how foreigners have them bluffed. Two days ago, coming from the South Bank in a sampan, I lost my wallet containing five hundred Chinese dollars. I didn't know it until I got home and changed my clothes. I couldn't remember the sampan coolie — they all look alike to me — or the number on his boat. I never pay any attention. But I got my money back. I simply went to the police and reported my loss. The next day, there was my wallet intact." He sighed. "But it wasn't always that way. Someone's cleaned up Chungking."

The Hatchet Man, I guessed. My students, divided as vice squads, had come back with revealing information, though I could see it was nothing new to them. For as long as twenty-four hours at a time, they had kept different enterprises of the underworld — opium joints, whorehouses, sing-song theaters, and beggars — under observation. Invariably they had seen these make payoffs to their masters. In class I learned from the students that a well-controlled city was directed by an underworld chief having no part in the police or city government. He was so powerful that the mayor, appointed by the Central Government in Chungking, had little to say in the city's government except to demand reasonable discretion in robberies, murder, and rape. To this the chief agreed. Thus, if in the robbery of a prominent tobacco store someone was killed, the mayor would demand an explanation of the chief — not for the theft, but for the murder. He, in turn, would demand an explanation of his lieutenant in that district. If this lieutenant could not find the murderer, he had to find someone else to offer for execution. The point was that robbery was a recognized trade, but if the robbers were so stupid as to kill someone of importance, one of the group had to be offered for sacrifice — usually one chosen by lot.

Every conceivable business or trade in Chungking was unofficially licensed through stooges of the chief, and all had to pay tribute to the association — theaters, opium joints, whores, beggars, ricksha coolies, sampan coolies, every retail and wholesale store, and every conceivable activity that produced income. Seeing this system unfold before me, I reflected on the advice of a Chinese who said, "If you wish to go in business in China, go in business with a Chinese."

"You got your money back," I said to Schwer, "because it was hot and the chief doesn't want to handle hot money."

"That's it."

"Then we foreigners are immune from Chinese robbers and murderers just as long as the Powers watch over us. Is that it?" I wondered uneasily how a Japanese assassin fitted into the picture.

"Absolutely," said Schwer.

"And if the Powers forget us?"

"A most unpleasant possibility," Schwer observed, and drew an expressive finger across his throat.

5

At the formal graduation exercises of the school for espionage, the diplomas were handed out by the Hatchet Man, flanked by a number of bigwigs from headquarters. Then without warning the Hatchet Man whispered to Ling, who told me blandly that I was to make a five-minute speech to the graduating class. Before I knew what had happened, I was on my feet on the rostrum, gazing vacantly at my fifty students, with Ling at my side to gather the pearls as they dropped from my lips.

I searched my mind for something worth saying, for some of the boys would go on dangerous missions behind the lines in occupied China. I bethought me of a harangue I had frequently given Ling and Wu on the Western philosophy of quick decisions and prompt action. In this vein I talked, illustrating my theme with such appropriate instances from history as I could recall. Napoleon's genius as an artillery officer, I averred, was no more than his habit of arriving at a given point a few minutes ahead of the enemy and with a greater weight of guns.

The applause evoked by this dubious bit of history was not enthusiastic, and when I was seated again I asked Ling how I had done.

"Not so hot," said Ling. "You insult Chinaman's ancient custom when you ask him to do today what he can always do tomorrow."

I would have thought little of my failure as a public speaker had it not been that, later, this characteristic bit of Chinese philosophy cost some of the students their lives. The Donkey planned to send ten of them through the lines disguised as coolies and carrying small sending radios patterned after those captured from parachuted Japanese spies around Chungking. I had insisted that the boys be parachuted at night from reconnaissance planes. But there were no parachutes immediately available. Whether or not the Donkey had ordered them made, they did not show up. So the radios were concealed in small clocks, at which I protested strenuously.

The boys themselves seemed unconcerned with the risks they ran, for though it is difficult to get middle-class Chinese into combat, they have great courage and accept missions that would curl the hair of a foreign combat soldier. As could have been anticipated, the Japanese searched the boys at the lines and, finding the clocks, were immediately suspicious. Of what possible use is a clock to a coolie — or to any other Chinese, for that matter? The Japanese examined the clocks, and the result was that ten brave men lost their heads.

As far as I could learn, there was more concern expressed over the loss of the radios than the heads.

· Chungking, November 1939

DESPITE MY HOMESICKNESS and desire to leave, I listened to the voice of the tempter and agreed to remain in Chungking another six months. Accordingly, I have signed a lease on the small apartment house immediately back of Schwer's and higher up the promontory, overlooking a small park and the yellow Yangtze. The city is again overcast with mist, which will probably remain until spring, making bombing difficult. Schwer and I thought to turn an honest dollar by renting our furnished space to foreigners, now that the city is filling up again and living quarters are at a premium. Yet scarcely was the ink dry on the lease than the Donkey appeared at my office and asked me how much space I was taking for myself.

I told him the third and fourth floors. Each of the first three floors has a large sitting room with two fireplaces and a balcony, two bedrooms with ample closets, a small room for storage, and a tiled bath, with a coke-heated boiler on the fourth floor to heat water. The top floor has a large Chinese cooking range and a number of rooms for servants. The walls are plastered and the floors are of pine. Most of the roofing tiles have been knocked off by falling debris from bombings, and all the glass in the windows has been shattered. The building is nevertheless in surprisingly good condition, considering the havoc caused in its vicinity by bombs and fires. To find the place at all, we had to climb over mountains of debris, but now the coolies have cleared a path up the narrow street to the entrance.

"I would like to have the first and second floors," the Donkey told me, Ling translating, and because I feared trouble if I refused, I agreed to his request. Schwer, I felt sure, would be willing to give up the venture.

"The general says that if you wish, the Service will take over the lease and make the necessary repairs. In this way you will be at no expense."

Also, I thought but did not say, the Donkey will go rent free, will get his food free from my kitchen, and all will be charged on the books to the upkeep of the foreign adviser.

Thus it was agreed. The building was already fairly well furnished with cheap native-made beds, chairs, tables, and the like. I moved the best of them to the third floor, brought in my box couch, which had been saved from the hut, and Ling bought a few native rugs, which were charged to the government. Wu made me more silk lamps — happily avoiding pink this time — and the Service gave me another gramophone and installed the best radio to be found in these parts. Altogether, with a few rat holes stopped and coke burning in each of my two small fireplaces, I was made quite comfortable again.

Now that the Donkey can keep his eye on me from the second floor, he feels much better. The two Service families that he moved in on the first floor also watch the comings and goings of the foreigner and his visitors. And there are, besides, two guards on duty at the entrance at all times.

"Can't we get rid of these guards?" I asked Ling.

"The Service pays them," said Ling. "What do you care?"

"I care a lot. I have to tip them every month, and getting kowtowed to when I come and go isn't worth the money."

"Not every foreigner is kowtowed to," Ling returned. "You are honored, Adviser."

"Not every foreigner pays for it, either," I grumbled.

I have a new houseboy, whom I selected from a group of servants at the chateau. He says no word of English but "orange juice," with which he greets me every time I get home and when

I ring for him in the morning. Oranges are plentiful, and I drink a half-gallon of juice every day. The Service got fed up with Lao Tsai, my former houseboy. A servant is allowed a reasonable squeeze or overcharge for everything he buys for the household. He gets this through agreements with merchants to charge 10 percent above the normal price. But Lao Tsai wasn't satisfied with this and padded the household expenses until he grew so rich that he became a moneylender to government clerks at exorbitant rates. His accounts when examined revealed that the Adviser was eating daily an average of six-dozen eggs, six pounds of pork, five loaves of bread, quantities of smuggled canned butter, costing $40 for twelve ounces, and smuggled canned milk at $10 a small tin. Now Lao Tsai is confined under guard on the chateau grounds and has been demoted to coolie status, at $9.00 a month and food, the usual pay.

Lao Han, the new boy, is cheerful and a hard worker. When I pointed this out to Ling, he shrugged and said, "Ancient custom is change servants every year. Familiarity breeds theft and laziness." Lao Han's wife is happy in her status of wife to a servant of the "foreign gentleman," and no longer washes my clothes. She is now a lady and has more time to lavish on her firstborn, a boy. She keeps his head shaved, except for a spot the size of a dime on top of his head, where she lets his hair grow long and braids it into a queue, after the manner of her male ancestors.

Squeeze isn't confined to houseboys, I discovered when I checked on the amount of gas I use each month. My normal quota is a drum of fifty gallons a month, generously added to if I run out, which my chauffeur always sees to it that I do. When I drive the car myself, I always get about twenty miles to the gallon, but he says he can get only ten miles. So the last drum I got I opened myself and sealed every time I took gas from it. But this did no good, for he secretly drained enough gas from the car so that I still averaged only ten miles to the gallon. Then I kept a record of mileage on the car every time it was used and of the reading on the gasoline gauge. The chauffeur avoided this checkup by breaking the speedometer. The gasoline he steals he can sell for $25 Chinese per gallon on the black market, which should net him a pretty penny. He goes in for big stakes and also is a moneylender, but the Service dares do nothing with him, because there are so few Chinese who can drive cars.

When I opened my gasoline drum I discovered six inches of space at the top. I asked Schwer about this, who said one inch was enough for expansion.

"Someone is stealing five gallons out of each drum before I get it," I said. "That's equal to a hundred and twenty-five Chinese dollars."

Schwer laughed. "And multiply that by thousands and thousands of drums of gasoline used by the government, and you get into real dough."

"I'll report this to my superiors," I said.

Schwer advised seriously against my doing so. Then it came home to me that this was not the petty graft of small fry but a gigantic squeeze by government officials, reminiscent of official theft in America.

I talked to Ling about it. He also was amused. "Small thief if caught is executed," said Ling. "If successful he becomes honored official, and bigger theft becomes perquisite of office."

Which philosophy recalls Western wisdom both ancient and modern to the same effect. Nor did it seem to me, on mature thought, that I was the one to initiate reforms in China.

2

While I was in the office a few days ago word came from the Donkey that I should return home at once. The matter was urgent.

"What's up?" I asked Ling and Wu.

They didn't know, but the Donkey came to my apartment a few moments after I arrived, evidently in quite a huff. He showed Ling and Wu a long cable from America. It was in both Chinese and English. Ling handed me the English version, saying, "Excerpts from the *New York Tribune*, with a Shanghai dateline."

So it was. I had been expecting something like this for some time, for sooner or later the correspondents must find something to say about me. Now, judging by the Donkey's demeanor, I was in for it.

I do not have the exact words, but the dispatch read something like this:

> SHANGHAI
> Information has leaked out of China that Major Herbert O. Yardley of Black Chamber fame is in Chungking unraveling Japanese code messages. Codeman Yardley, it is said, is working for the Generalissimo under an assumed name.

The dispatch shifted to Washington and continued:

> The Department of State, when interviewed, declared that Yardley applied for a passport in 1938 to travel in the British Empire as an importer. They denied knowledge of his present whereabouts.

When I returned the paper to Ling, the Donkey looked at me angrily.

"What of it?" I said to Ling. "I've always told you my presence was no more than a Chinese secret."

Ling made no reply to this, and I asked Wu to translate to the Donkey what I had said. The Donkey's concern, it appeared from his reply, was less for my safety than for his own neck should I be assassinated by the Japanese, in which case he would be held responsible.

"Tell the general," I said to Wu, "that everyone here knows who I am."

"The general asks," Wu returned, "how anyone can know your name."

"Well," I said, "to enumerate a few: since I have been here

there have been eight different guards, three chauffeurs, four houseboys, four wash *amahs,* and three cooks. Servants gossip."

"The general says servants would not dare gossip."

"The chauffeur I shot doesn't care for me."

"He wouldn't talk, the general says."

"Someone at the chateau stole my typewriter, some of my papers, including my passport in the name of Yardley, and all of Ling's clothes. I suppose the thief won't talk for pay!" I added sarcastically.

"The general says the thief was one of the house servants, who was caught and executed and your effects returned."

I was resolved not to be outargued in this foolish dispute.

"Direct the general's attention to the headquarters sign in Chinese on my car and the fact that my chauffeur is usually in uniform."

"The general says no one knows what the sign says."

"It is the same sign used by all Chinese generals in the Service," I remarked acidly.

The Donkey digested this and started on a new tack.

"The general thinks you associate too much with foreigners," Wu translated.

Having argued this subject often, I refused to be drawn again, and the Donkey talked on.

"He says this dispatch was written by a foreigner and how could a foreigner know if you didn't tell him."

"Correspondents come and go," I said. "If a newspaper thought I was in Chungking — and many persons in America know I am, for I write to them — the correspondent need only look for a bald-headed man with the second finger on his right hand missing."

I had struck the right note at last. The Donkey was clearly impressed and went into a long conversation with Wu and Ling.

"The general suggests," Wu said gravely, "that the Adviser wear an artificial finger to prevent identification."

"What!" I said. "No wig?"

"He hasn't thought of that yet."

"Let's get over with this foolishness," I said. "Surely he must realize that, since my identity has been officially verified, it's too late for concealment."

The Donkey has been mollified. A bald head and a missing finger rather than any carelessness or negligence on the part of the Chinese have led to my identification. The Donkey will sit up half the night elaborating the point in an official document to his superiors. Perhaps he will make copies of this for various bureaus and one for his own files. He will do this with black paint and a brush in his own hand. All officialdom becomes involved in red tape and suffocates under its own documents, but the Chinese, without the aid of Dictaphones, duplicating machines, and other devices, are peculiarly lost in their own memoranda. They must already be years and decades in arrears of events. One can visualize the governmental departments of the future steadily losing ground, until eventually the morning memorandum on the desk of an executive will have to do with events that occurred in his grandfather's time and the Chinese ideal of identification of the living with their dead ancestors will be wholly realized.

3

Ling has looked downcast all day, so when the general left, I asked him the trouble.

"Lao Shih is very sick with diphtheria," he said, "and I'm afraid the others will catch it."

Most Chinese do not give their children names until they are grown, referring to them meanwhile in the order of their birth — Lao Ta, Lao Ehr, Lao San, Lao Shih (Old One, Old Two, Old Three, Old Four). Lao Shih, fourth born, was just a year old.

"Besides," Ling continued, "Lao Wu is on the way."

"Four is too many, much less five," I said.

Said Ling ruefully, "Chinese Wisdom says: 'Deliver sons for old age; store up rice for famine.' "

"You'll have no sons for old age if you don't have them inoculated."

"I am not a rich man, Adviser."

"I told you I'd pay for it."

"You've already been too kind."

"How much will it cost?"

"Several hundred Chinese. The Chinese dollar gets thinner each day, and foreign medicine is prohibitive to Chinese."

"Is that why I saw you gambling with the chauffeur? Trying to win enough? And you lost instead."

"More than I could afford — half of the pay I got today."

I said, "There's plenty of easy money to be got in the poker game at the Chungking Hostel. Want me to risk fifty dollars for you?"

He looked in his pocketbook with a long face but handed me fifty dollars.

The Hostel is near the site of my former hut. It is a cheap structure of wood and plaster with a small amount of brick, originally built as a hospital. When foreigners began to flock to Chungking, the government turned it into a hotel, with living quarters for foreigners only, but with dining room open to all. There is a large lounge with radio and a stove, a large bare dining room, a few rooms for private parties, and a number of unheated bedrooms. As at the Café de la Paix in Paris, at the Hostel sooner or later one sees everyone worth knowing — foreign advisers, correspondents, businessmen, diplomats, as well as spies, crooks, whores, and expatriates. They come to eat foreign chow, such as it is, sip tea or a drink, play a game of bridge or poker, flirt, or merely drift in and out because of sheer ennui.

I had often dropped in at night for an expensive drink of smuggled Scotch and watched the poker game in one of the private rooms on the ground floor. I had never played, however, and truth is I was rather shocked at the casual method of play. I have heard it is the accepted style in the Orient and, if so, the card sharks have overlooked a lucrative field. To be sure, it takes a lot of Chinese dollars to buy anything, and the stakes are in Chinese money — bundles of it. At the Hostel the play is slovenly. They pay no attention to the rules as I know them and often make new ones on the spot to cover a disagreement. With childish, wishful thinking, they disregard all mathematical percentages; they bet Chinese money as if it had no value whatsoever, though to get it they must convert gold into Chinese. And to my horror they throw in their discards face up! They break all precepts on how to win at poker as known in my youth to all youngsters who frequented the eleven saloons and three poolrooms of Worthington, Indiana. Old Salty East and Mont Mull, in whose poker games I had cut my eyeteeth, simply would have passed out at the prospect of such an easy game as is afforded by the Chungking Hostel.

When I entered with Ling, a number of players were already at the table: snobbish, curly-headed Morgan Crofton, a British embassy code clerk who talked about going back to England to fight but did nothing about it; Ted White, a good-natured young reporter from *Time* who hoped someday to write a book; a boyish Chinese lad, foreign-dressed, suave, and diplomatic, called Ping, doubtless a spy on the foreigners; a pretty blond young Polish girl named Maya, married to a Chinese officer in Warsaw. Like Zelda, she had been reduced to the status of a concubine and had rebelled. She now worked for the Chinese government, broadcasting in French at unholy hours of the morning, and also, doubtless, reporting useless information about foreigners to the government. There was Stoney, a pleasant Irishman, and Gilbert, a quarrelsome Britisher, both having something to do with the Chinese salt taxes.

Stoney was checking out as I came in, so I took his seat, placing Ling's money before me while he sat uneasily in a corner. They were playing a bastard game of dealer's choice —

high-low, stud, draw, deuces wild, and what-not. I had been taught that in a steady grind of poker it is not what you win but what you save that puts you in the black. So, sticking to this principle, I played percentages carefully. Also, at home we never drew to less than a queen in the hole at five-card stud. But these foreign exiles in primitive China drew to a deuce, to inside straights, to three-card flushes, and to almost anything, as long as they could occupy their minds and forget their lot. And, as I said, they threw in their cards face up. Since I was out to win Ling a few hundred dollars, I thought I might as well take advantage of all this and get the operation over as quickly as possible.

Most persons successful in cryptography have what is known as a photographic mind. Otherwise, they could not retain the long sequences of code words and letters that they must remember if they are to solve their problems. This is not memory; it is mental photography. I could retain long sequences of cards, and when dealing, I had no trouble at all gathering the turned-up cards, placing them in the bottom of the deck, and making a few false shuffles, carefully taught me by Salty and Mont, so that when the cards were cut at least a large part of the sequence was at the top of the deck. Then when I dealt I called for five-card stud, which meant that when I looked at my hole card at the first round, I knew the hole card of the other players. Also, if a few dropped out, leaving the play to those who had done the betting, I could calculate pretty accurately in advance who, if anyone, was going to help his hand.

I do not mean to say that I can do much with a deck of cards. Certainly I cannot emulate Mont, who, in his youth, sat hours each day at a table set with mirrors and only when he could not see himself cheat felt qualified to play in any company, even in Worthington, Indiana. He had large hands, and mine are small, and besides, I have lost a finger. Yet even so, in this company I felt I could chisel out a few hundred for Ling.

Morgan Crofton, the English code clerk holding a job I had

graduated from at half his age, had taken an intense dislike to me and, when I dealt, always overbet in the attempt to run me out. If the sequence of cards I had mentally photographed indicated that he had the better hand, I threw in my cards; otherwise, I raised him unmercifully at each card. At each loss he became increasingly nasty, and Ling, seeing his $50 gradually increase to $1000, broke out in a sweat, though the room was cold and damp.

For a while the game was interrupted when a striking, black-haired woman in a mink coat came in to watch. She was more than plump, and she was smoking a huge black cigar. I had never seen her before, but when Morgan, Ted, and Ping fluttered about her and called her Mickey, I knew she must be Emily Hahn, who, gossip said, was in Chungking to write the history of the three Soong sisters, Mmes. Chiang, Kung, and Sun.

Drinks were ordered and the game was resumed, peacefully enough until Morgan, having two aces exposed at the third card, raised me $200 Chinese, scaring the others out and leaving just us two. I had a pair of fives exposed and a queen in the hole. Unless my mental picture had failed me, his hole card was a ten. Also, if I was not mistaken, he would not help his hand but at the fifth card I would draw a queen, giving me queens and fives against his pair of aces. With his fourth card he bet $500 and I merely called, for I was afraid that, despite his English denseness, he might catch on and demand the cards be cut.

Ling, perspiring freely and now the color of old ivory, rose from his seat and looked on breathlessly. I gave him a wink, but he could manage only a sickly grin in return. I reflected that I'd be sick myself if somehow I had made a mistake.

At the fifth card Morgan emptied his pockets and I called. Over $3000 Chinese was on the table. When I showed him two pairs and — because of his insolence — dragged in the money even before he turned his hole card, he angrily tore up the cards.

"I'll play with you no more!" he cried, flushed and shaking. Then he paused and, to make his words more dramatic, curled his lips and sneered, *"Mister Herbert Osborn Yardley!"*

He waited for something to happen, but no one so much as cracked a smile.

"Let's get out of here, Mickey," he said and left with her, she unperturbed and still puffing at her big black cigar.

I picked up the money to go.

"Bloody ass," said Ping. "Pay no attention. Sit down and play, Osborn."

"See you some other time," I said, a bit conscience-stricken, for I had taken some of his money as well as that of others, and they all, after the custom of the Orient, had been decent enough not to inquire about me in public. But, I reflected, it was all in a good cause.

Outside, I thrust my winnings and Ling's original stake into his hands.

Tears of gratitude were in his eyes, and it seemed to me true that on occasion the end justifies the means.

To break the tension I said, "What did you think of Miss Hahn? The boys seem to like her."

Now himself, Ling grinned. "Old Chinese saying, 'When no tiger in mountain, then monkey is king.' "

· Chungking, January 1940

I HAVE WRITTEN NO WORD for a long time. Also, I've about given up fighting my lot. It does no good. Long ago I sent wireless operators and Japanese translators with equipment to the fronts, east, north, south. All to no avail. They are too cowardly to remain close enough to the front to intercept long-wave messages for study and decipherment. They make a gesture but never stay long, and when recalled and asked the reason, they say that the troops were retreating and they were afraid they would lose their equipment to the enemy. I have hounded headquarters to let me go to one of the fronts, but thus far have received evasive answers. We can, of course, receive shortwave messages here in Chungking, but what is needed are front-line dispatches, which, for technical reasons, are sent long wave. Such messages can be heard only near the scene of battle, and the Chinese hate nothing worse than gunfire. I'll not tolerate the situation much longer.

I'm very snug in my apartment, and thinking to give a Christmas Eve party to some foreign friends, I bought six ducks to fatten. I penned them on the servants' balcony, Lao Han, my boy, helping, with instructions to stuff them with all the wet rice they would eat. I even bought soy-bean curd for them, thinking it would give me a sort of milk-fed duck, such as we have in Indiana. After three weeks, the breasts of the ducks were still as flat as before. I don't know whether the Chinese duck is skinny by nature or whether the servants ate the rice and bean curd. So I gave up the Christmas Eve party and went instead to a Service dinner, where I was showered with gifts and *kampeied* into the small hours. I surprised them with ice cream made from smuggled canned milk and frozen in Neilson's handmade freezer.

2

A young chap I shall call Hugh, from the American embassy, woke me up at ten on Christmas morning. I had seen him at the Chungking Club across the river and now and then at the Hostel and had taken a liking to him because of his sense of humor and lack of pretense and inhibition.

He had a Chinese girl with him who giggled when I got out of bed and put on a bathrobe. Lao Han brought a pot of coffee, a product of Neilson's handmade coffee roaster, and when I served it, she stood up and bowed and thanked me, Chinese fashion. The spoon seemed to bother her, but otherwise she was at ease.

"She's on her way to Chengtu to college," Hugh told me. "I spoke to her in a teahouse and told her to follow me here. Hope you don't mind."

Hugh spoke good Mandarin but was easily taken in by girls. Rumor was that college students could be had for a price, but I was always skeptical. More likely, it seemed to me, Chinese whores were getting wise to the ways of foreigners and pretended to be "family" girls in distress.

"You'll be wanting my spare bedroom?" I asked.

"A hot bath for her too" — he grinned — "but there's no hurry."

I'd thought sometimes I might be better off as a procurer than by being so damned accommodating. I slept on my box couch in the large living room, which gave me two extra bedrooms; foreigners, seeing such luxury, usually hinted that they could use them to advantage, if I didn't mind. To one not living in Chungking, where privacy is almost unknown, such a hint might seem out of order. But I, who had fought for privacy, appreciated their plight and, being easygoing by nature, had agreed to most of the sly hints of the less snobbish foreigners. But it may be that I am not by nature easygoing. On reflection, I think my motives are more likely engendered by curiosity. Perhaps I wanted to know how many foreigners are frauds in their sex life, such as it is in Chungking. All, I noted, looked with envy at my spare bedroom. After this I could usually count on a chit asking me to lunch. This became so routine that I grinned to myself while they talked about everything else but Chinese women. Then the luncheon would end up with a proposition. I looked like a good fellow. How about lending my key some afternoon? Or, "I'm going to the front with the propaganda minister, Hollington Tong, and when I get back will leave for the States, but before I go I'd like to sleep with a Chinese girl. I must find out if what they say at home is really true. Could you find me one?"

In Chungking, especially in winter, when there are no bombings to keep one occupied, one will do most anything for diversion. For those I liked, I picked out a sing-song girl with the help of Fidelity's friend who was married to the gambler. For some reason I called her Miss Wang and introduced her suitors as Mr. Wang. "Miss Wang, meet Mr. Wang," I would always say in Chinese, which got a smile from her. She has a steady income and has met many Mr. Wangs — newsmen, military attachés, gunboat officers, and once a diplomat. She sings nicely and, with a few drinks of yellow wine, accompanies her songs with graceful gestures. But she is a lady and needs to be courted on a grand style, so I always order dinner for her and her intended from nearby teahouses and, with the admonition to Mr. Wang that her price is $200 Chinese and that he should pay Lao Han for the dinner with a generous tip for him and for the wash *amah,* who will have to wash the sheets and pillow slips, I leave the Wangs to their new happiness.

On one occasion on my return to my apartment I had seen

Mr. Wang, a visiting military attaché, naked in the bathroom, washing himself with whiskey.

"Haven't you a prophylactic?" I asked.

"Old army method good enough for me," he said.

But even less practical was a newsman. He was tight when I got back, and he was singing with Miss Wang. He had taken no precautions at all and seemed insulted when I sent Ling after something.

"She's a nice girl," I said, "but she's probably got the clap."

This had sobered him up enough to thank Ling for his kindness, which Ling accepted sullenly, for he feels shame for his race, which stoops to have intercourse with the white man, and shame also for the Honorable Adviser, who encourages it even to lending his apartment. He once said angrily, "You wouldn't let a friend in New York bring a girl to your apartment. Why do you do it in China?"

But when I told him I would, he was unconvinced and said I lost face. "You know how much I care about that," I had said.

Hugh, my embassy friend, had turned on the gramophone and was dancing with his Chinese friend.

"What goes on at the embassy?" I asked.

"Nothing. They're still squawking to Washington about the Japanese bombing last fall. Near bomb hits on the embassy here, destruction of missionary property, a few deaths. That sort of thing."

"What does Washington say?"

"You ought to know. They've protested to Japan."

"Why complain about bombings?" I asked. "Why not complain about selling steel, airplane engines, and gasoline to the Japanese?"

"No use in that," he said, eyeing his girl covetously. "Foreign exports and all that sort of thing. You know the crowd."

"Maybe a little fun might help." I looked at his companion. "Chinese girl, for instance."

"Lose face," he said.

"There're no women at the embassy," I said. "What do they do for women?"

"They don't. They stay at home and masturbate — embassy's favorite indoor sport. That reminds me" — he laughed — "the Chinese have a word for it: 'naughty.' "

"Naughty in Chinese is *wan pi,*" I said.

"Sure, *wan pi,* play skin. Even girls say *Ni shih wan pi,* you is play skin."

"I'll run along," I said, "and let you two play with each other."

He kissed his companion, and as I left I saw her, Chinese fashion, wiping her mouth.

3

There is a Shanghai sing-song theater here that miraculously escaped destruction in the bombings. It is run by the mama and papa of a family with eight children, three of them beautiful daughters who are actresses. This theater is a bit different from the run of sing-song theaters in Chungking. These ordinarily have a Chinese orchestra composed of one-string fiddles, tom-toms, and ear-splitting brasses. A Chinese girl enters the stage and, to the accompaniment of the orchestra, sings through her nose in a high, squealing voice and with no play of facial expression or pantomime. If the customers like her, they momentarily stop chewing watermelon seeds and yell *Yao-ti ma* and *Hao hao,* and if she is in a good humor she will gargle her throat from a teapot, spit copiously on the stage, and re-enact the crime.

To ensure an encore, you give one of the ushers $10 Chinese for her. This may also entitle you to an introduction to her *amah* owner, and if you look prosperous you may have tea in the singer's room. If you are set on making a conquest, you appear the next night and this time give the *amah* $10, and after the girl sings her regular song the stagehand hangs up a sign indicating a "request" number, which demonstrates the singer's popularity and raises the price of her favors. This may go on for several days in order to whet your desire, and finally, if the *amah* approves, for a price you may take the singer home with you.

This Shanghai outfit is different. The music is provided by a long-armed banjo, which emits not-unpleasing chords, and the singer or singers are skilled in pantomime, so the act is altogether pleasing.

Wu, Ling, and I, being bored after the day's work, began to attend this Shanghai theater. Often we went home with Mama and Papa and the three daughters, whom we dubbed the Three Virgins. They lived at the river's edge in a bamboo hut built on stilts above the high-water mark.

The Three Virgins were not to be had for a night but were up for marriage or for purchase as concubines. Either would entail feeding, clothing, and housing them indefinitely. Wu, in the presence of the Three Virgins, spun a long yarn about me: that I was a wealthy merchant with a kind heart who wished to purchase a concubine. The Three Virgins, ages sixteen, eighteen, and nineteen, beamed. The other five children, all quite young, peeped through the cracks in the walls and giggled. Papa, scenting a customer, sent out for a jug of yellow wine. The Virgins themselves drank only tea and were too ladylike to smoke. On the slightest provocation they arose to fill our cups or light our cigarettes. It was all too painfully genteel for words. The talk, too, was of everything but the price, until Wu made discreet inquiries and was told the foreigner must come again before the matter could be discussed.

We came again after going to the theater and asking for "request" numbers at $10 each. After much ceremonious palaver, Papa then said he would require $4000 Chinese deposited in the bank to his account and $3000 in the daughter's account.

"Tell Papa," I said to Wu, "I don't want to buy the whole family." Wu was too good a Chinese to give offense by obeying me. So we left without further bargaining, to return two weeks later. This interval served to soften up the old man, who now said the price was $3000 for him and $2000 for the girl, a net reduction of $2000. Mama, animated by the prospective sale of a daughter, now smiled and asked which one I wanted. Wu said in Chinese, "The youngest."

This I understood and said no, I wanted the eldest, Number One. Mother complimented me on my good taste, saying the youngest, Number Three, was a problem child, whereas the eldest was kind and even-tempered and obedient. Thereupon, Virgins Number Two and Number Three left the room in a huff, and Number One beamed at me. She can't get away from Mama, I thought, but once she is the foreigner's concubine, she'll see her lover easily enough.

Five thousand dollars Chinese is about $200 gold. Wu now told them the foreigner must consider the matter, saying this was a great deal of money. Then he asked, "How can the foreigner know the eldest has never been with men?"

Mama declared brightly she could guarantee virginity — her daughters had never left her sight. Despite this assurance, I was somewhat skeptical. However, I asked Number One if she wished to come and live with me. She nodded vigorously and said, *"Shih-ti, shih-ti."*

We prepared to leave, whereupon a look of disappointment crossed the faces of Papa, Mama, and Number One, and an animated conversation involving Wu and Ling ensued.

"They agree now to come down a thousand," Wu informed me. "That makes the price four thousand dollars."

"Tell them," I said in my most businesslike manner, "that the foreigner must consider the matter," and after much kowtowing, we left.

Some time later we went to the theater to resume negotiations. The Three Virgins sang and Mama accepted my money for request numbers. But we were not invited to accompany them home. The Three Virgins, it appeared, no longer lived with their parents. I had missed the boat. At the bargain price of $4000 each the Three Virgins had been sold as a team to a dizzy American aviator who had come here to demonstrate an American pursuit plane. However, they brought him bad luck, for a crowd of us won $70,000 Chinese from him in a crap game. As one of the winners, and regretting lost opportunities, I offered him $3000 for Number One, now slightly shop-worn. He said it was a deal and I should give him the $3000. I said I wanted an IOU. So he wrote me one reading, "IOU Virgin No. One — price $3000 Mex," and signed his name.

It was agreed he could redeem his pledge that night if he got lucky. It never fails. Lend a fellow money in a card or crap game, and he'll clean you out. He didn't quite do that, but he won back half of his $70,000 and redeemed his IOU to me.

Perhaps it was just as well, for if I had acquired Number One, I'd have had to feed her forever. The only way to be rid of such an obligation is to leave town.

· Chungking, April 1940

ANOTHER BIRTHDAY COME AND GONE, this one celebrated at
the Hatchet Man's with many *kam-peis* of imported brandy. I
feel myself growing old in China. No longer can I drink these
Chinese under the table. Schwer also threw me a party at Pop
Neilson's place. There were two faces new to me: one, a shy
little Chinese girl, possibly nine years old, named Ing-ing; and
a beautiful blond German girl of twenty-one named Maria.
Both have sad histories.

An American sailor shacked up with a Chinese across the
Yangtze. The custom of having a kept woman is permitted by
the American gunboat officers to keep the boys out of worse
mischief, provided they bring the girl to the gunboat for a
physical examination. If the girl doesn't run a positive Wasser-
man, which I am told most of them do because of inherited
syphilis, the union is blessed. In this case, to ensure herself
against old age, the girl took the money the sailor gave her and
purchased Ing-ing from a passing Yangtze junk. A wise *amah*
can reap a fortune from wealthy Chinese merchants and high
officials by selling them a child virgin for a night. The child is
carefully schooled to cry as though with pain even after many
intimacies with many men so that she can be sold repeatedly
as a virgin at fancy prices. The sailor became attached to pretty
Ing-ing, and when her *amah* owner offered her to a merchant,
the sailor purchased the child and gave her written freedom. He
sent her to Pop's, where she was to be educated by private

tutors and lead a normal childhood. Then the sailor was suddenly transferred, and Pop, grown fond of Ing-ing, gave her a
home in the compound as his adopted daughter. She adores
Pop, but inasmuch as she prefers the company of prostitutes to
tutors, he is having a task in making a lady of her.

Maria's parents were well-to-do Germans in Berlin. Her
brother was one of the first four hundred Hitler surrounded
himself with. In Paris, studying music, at the age of eighteen
she met a young Chinese who swept her off her feet with his
lavish attentions. They were married in Paris, and a year later
her husband returned with her to his home in Chengtu, where
he soon took a Chinese wife and reduced Maria to the status
of servant-concubine. On her marriage, Maria not only lost her
citizenship, but her family disowned her. Her husband had
taken her money and "invested" it for her. There were no
children. Her eyes having been opened to the life of degradation
that would be hers in China, she sold her rings, gathered a few
clothes, and flew to Chungking. Here she hoped the German
ambassador would protect her from Chinese-wife law, restore
her citizenship, and secure her parents' forgiveness. But she had
received scant encouragement, and her, too, Pop had taken in
and treated like a daughter.

As we returned from the birthday party, Schwer said, "Maria
is going to give German lessons." Then, with a sly wink, "Why
don't you improve your German? She speaks good French,
too." When I made no comment, he added, "Her English is
poor. Maybe you can swap English for German and French
lessons."

So later it was arranged. But Maria in her new profession as
language teacher made very little money, and I saw to it that
she was put on the Chinese payroll. All the stranded girls in
Chungking were taking money either from amorous males or
from the government. I don't know what possible use they can
be to China, but it is a kindly dispensation, for if the girls wish
to remain physically honest, they can do so.

About a week ago I took Maria to dinner and a Chinese movie. When I got her back to Pop's compound about ten o'clock, Pop was waiting up for her and gave me a sour look, which brightened when he won a drink off me at dice. Then he gave me one on the house. After that I left, and the next day there was a false alarm of a bombing raid. Immediately after the all-clear signal, Maria appeared at my apartment in tears.

"Pop's dead," she said in French. "I have no friend now." He had dropped dead at the entrance to a bomb shelter.

The Germans, though divided into factions, united to give Pop an impressive burial. Many other foreigners, old-timers in Chungking, and many Chinese paid him tribute, too. I prayed for no bombs so that the old fellow who so feared raids could be buried in peace. The casket, covered with flowers, was borne on bamboo poles by coolies to a burial plot near the Hostel. But not one newsman had even heard of Pop, known and loved by nearly everyone who knows Chungking at all. Nor did any missionary come to pay him respect, for to missionaries he was an evil man who kept an evil place.

Ing-ing was nowhere about. She had not been seen since Pop's death. But at his empty grave we found her, sad but dry-eyed.

The German consul officiated and gave Pop what I took to be a Nazi burial. At any rate, when the casket was lowered each German passed, tossed three handfuls of dirt into the grave, saluted, and said, *"Heil Hitler."* Pop, a Dane and not a German, would have stroked his Vandyke and chuckled, could he have seen.

When the ceremony was over, Pop's servants tried to get Ing-ing to go back with them. She stubbornly shook her head. She watched the coolies fill the grave, and when they had gone, she still remained, squatted on the ground.

Maria, with no guardian, went to live at the German consulate compound next to the Hostel with another German girl who also had married a Chinese. Ing-ing came and went from Pop's compound for several days. I told Wu and Ling about her, and they said they could find a good home for her. We all went to tell her the good news.

Wu and Ling talked at length with the servants. One was crying.

"What do they say?" I asked.

"They say," Ling said, "the prostitutes have stolen Ing-ing."

Chungking, May 1940

ON MY RETURN TO CHUNGKING from the front, I ran into the German Jew who was on the small tramp freighter that took me from Hong Kong to Haiphong, Indo-China. He had taken motion pictures of the coast, at Pakhoi, and along the French railway running through Indo-China to Kunming, China. Though he had posed as an engineer on his way to China to examine mines for Shanghai interests, he was, I thought, far too curious about Chinese communications. I had no proof, but it seemed likely he was working for Japan, despite his status as a refugee. Here in Chungking I found him stopping at the Hostel but avoiding the dining room and not mixing with foreigners. He let it be known that he preferred the downtown Chinese restaurants. He could scarcely be blamed for that, the fare at the Hostel being none too good, consisting mostly of chicken with black skin. Why an inscrutable providence has granted the people of China yellow skins and their chickens black is a subject I should like to explore.

Out of idle curiosity — or perhaps on a hunch — one day while the boy was absent from the registration desk I turned back the pages until I found his name. To my amazement, I found he was registered as a Honduran subject, naturalized in 1938. It was common knowledge that citizenship in Honduras together with a fancy passport could be purchased in Paris if one had the money. The refugee, I thought, would bear watching.

A bit later we heard a new type of wireless signals, rather weak and hand-sent. The sender did not call a station. The messages were short and in figures and were without address or signature. There was no acknowledgment. They were usually repeated twice and sent at irregular intervals and at irregular times, making the location of the wireless sending apparatus most difficult with our limited equipment and personnel. There was some indication that the place of sending was in the German consulate, whose compound was within a hundred yards of the Hostel. Maria was living with a German girl in the compound, and because of my association with Maria, this fact became highly embarrassing to me. However, I didn't know the matter was serious until one day Wu said, "The Donkey swears the messages are from the German compound. He thinks Maria is a Japanese spy working through the Germans."

I laughed. "Maria doesn't know a thing."

"He hints," said Wu gravely, "that you, too, may be implicated."

I said, "You're pulling my leg."

But Wu said no, and that the Donkey was both more stupid and more dangerous than I knew. Also that I'd better do something about it.

But what could I do? I couldn't decipher the messages. There were too few of them and they were too short to provide sufficient material for analysis. But the character of the messages suggested that they might be test messages, such as would be sent by one seeking contact with his correspondent and thus far unsuccessfully. This could be, if the signals were too weak. The messages were unanswered, as far as we could detect.

"You'll do something, won't you, Adviser?" Wu asked.

"What would you recommend? That I escape before I'm arrested?"

"Either find the wireless or decipher the messages," said Wu.

"You know the German Jew I told you about in confidence,

the chap who stays at the Hostel? He's a more likely suspect than Maria, who's far too dumb to be a spy."

"You think the wireless is in the Hostel instead of the German compound?"

"It could be," I said.

We got out the charts showing lines drawn on the map of Chungking from various points where our direction finders had beamed the strange signals. The lines converged at several points, all in the general area of the German compound, which included also the Hostel. Wu is an engineer of sorts and since he came to me has studied wireless signals a bit. He agreed that it could just as well be the Hostel as the German compound.

"But it will be hard to prove," Wu said.

"Not if you don't mind mosquito bites," I answered. "I'd do it myself, but I'd be recognized."

"Do what?"

"Well, the signals are always sent at night, and at night coolies sleep on the ground all over Chungking. After dark you could put on coolie clothes and lie on the ground near the entrance to the Chungking dugout. No one would disturb you or pay any notice. You could take my direction finder, wrap it in some old clothes, and, once you were settled in the dark, try to pick up the signals. It might be several nights before you heard them. But once you did, we'd know whether the signals came from the German compound or the Hostel. The direction finder is accurate enough to determine that."

"I'm willing to try," said Wu, "if only to confound the Donkey."

It was agreed that Wu should start that night, armed with a bottle of quinine to offset the mosquitoes, and for three nights he underwent his ordeal. A little after midnight each evening I drove out to the Hostel and managed to get close to him, unobserved. I'd kid him a bit and then slip him a small bottle of brandy. The brandy didn't deter the mosquitoes, but, as Wu said, it helped one to be philosophical and probably the Ancient

Wisdom came about in some such way: Confucius and the rest, bitten by various insects, took to drink. From alcohol was born proverbial philosophy.

On the third night, around daylight, Wu came to my apartment, sweating profusely because of his haste, but grinning happily.

"You were right!" he said. "And the Donkey is nuts. The direction finder pointed straight at the Hostel. There was a short message around four o'clock on thirteen kilocycles. It was all in figures like the others, but the signals are now much stronger."

"You got the message?"

"No, I didn't bother. But I know this is what you want."

"Good," I said. "I'll recommend you for the Dragon Cross, or Knight of the Bath for Sing-Song Girls."

Wu was willing to settle for a drink and a few hours' sleep, after which I outlined a plan. He was to search all the Chinese records to find out what baggage the refugee had carried on his arrival. I then wrote an urgent note to Maria to come to my apartment, and sent it by my chauffeur.

Wu returned before Maria arrived and found me filing picklocks from steel wire.

"The refugee came via CNAC from Kunming," Wu said. "The records indicate he had a very small trunk and three suitcases."

Maria came running, all out of breath. "Oo la la," she said, fanning herself. "Vat you vant, so early night?"

I told her I'd found her a nice safe place to live, across the Yangtze. She had outworn her welcome at the German compound and was very happy at my news. I said I'd send my chauffeur back with her and that she could pack and bring her things here. Then, after the sun had set and it was cooler, we'd cross over.

She agreed readily, but I wasn't sure of her reaction when she had returned with her few poor belongings and I prepared to put my proposition to her. I poured her a drink by way of prelude.

"Maria," I said, "would you like to make enough money to take you to Shanghai?"

She had often told me that if she could get to Shanghai, friends there might be able to reach her brother in Germany, who, if he understood her plight, would intercede to have her German citizenship restored. As a Chinese citizen, she had practically no rights, being a woman. As a German citizen, she could defy her husband and secure a divorce.

"Oh, yes," she said in French, "what must I do?"

"Nothing dishonorable, I hope. I'll tell you later. But first I want you to stay here at the apartment. Eat and sleep here for a few days and don't leave without me. It won't be for long."

"All right," she agreed.

"You know what they'll say around town," I cautioned her; "that you're my mistress."

She shrugged. "They say that already." And then in English, "Go the hell mits 'em."

"You know the German Jew at the Hostel?" I asked.

"Der Schweinhund!"

"Spoken like a Nazi's sister. Well, his room is next to the ladies' room upstairs. I'll take you to the Hostel. It's siesta time now and almost everyone will be asleep. I want you to knock at his door, and if there's no answer, to unlock his door with this skeleton key and have a quick look at his baggage to see what kind of locks it has." I gave her the skeleton key I had made, a sort of master key for the locks used at the Hostel.

"I don't know anything about locks," she said.

All I wanted to know at the moment was whether the refugee's baggage had the ordinary cheap locks or the better type with tumblers. Later I would ask her to open his baggage and see if a radio set was inside. I'd have to train her for this. If the locks were of the ordinary type, the training would be simple. If tumbler locks, I'd need to give her longer schooling and make a different set of tools. Wu, who was watching, had brought an ordinary door lock. She tried the master key and locked and unlocked it easily.

"Suppose I get caught?" she asked.

"If he comes to the door when you knock, you say you're sorry, wrong door, and go on. If someone sees you, open the door. They'll think he gave you the key for a rendezvous."

"*Gott in Himmel!*" she cried, and then laughed. "All right, I will do it."

I showed her the difference between ordinary baggage locks and those with tumblers. Then the three of us set off for the Hostel. We had a drink in the lounge to give me time to look around. Everybody seemed to be asleep but one houseboy.

"All right, Maria," I said. "Time to go."

She nervously gulped her cocktail and went upstairs. When she returned a few minutes later, we joined her in the lobby and went to the car.

"Well?" I asked.

She held her hand over her heart. Her face was flushed and dripping with perspiration. I thought she might have had trouble.

"Anyone see you?" I asked.

She shook her head. "No, but I was frightened. I knocked, and when no one answered, I unlocked the door. I looked at his baggage, one small trunk and three suitcases. The trunk and one suitcase were unlocked. The other two were locked. The locks were like mine, the usual kind."

"Did you look inside those that were unlocked?"

"No," she said with a frown. "Should I have?"

"You did fine. Now we'll go home and practice opening locks."

"You think I can learn?"

"Sure," I said. "You're a clever girl."

She was certainly pretty but none too clever, I thought. However, I was taking no chances that she might be. I wasn't going to let her out of my sight until the case was completed. It wasn't that I was afraid, really, of being double-crossed, but once she had a few drinks, she became talkative. Her drinking would be with Wu and me.

There were five of my own suitcases at home and three of Maria's. While I showed her how to open them, Wu looked on.

"I'm glad they're not tumbler locks," I said, noting her awkwardness.

"Can you open tumbler locks with these two gadgets?" Wu asked with a smirk.

I rather thought he was alluding to my car and how at times I made off with it.

"Not with those," I said, "but with another kind."

"I'd like to learn." He grinned. "Maybe I might need the car some time."

"Perhaps some time I'll show you," I said, "but it takes a great skill and long training."

"Uh-huh," said Wu skeptically.

For two hours Maria worked diligently, opening and closing the locks over and over again, until her fingers were adept.

"I can do it in my sleep," she said, laughing.

Everything was now set until there was an air raid. I thought it better to wait until all the lights were off and the Hostel crowd gathered in the dugout, thus ensuring Maria plenty of time.

On the third day, after dinner, there was an alarm and we three drove to the Hostel, the pick-locks in Maria's purse, together with a pencil flashlight. We sat outside, where there are small tables, sipping drinks, while she complained bitterly.

There was the usual crowd — a few newsmen, missionaries, and businessmen, together with the Chinese who had come to seek safety in the dugout. The refugee was nowhere about, but there were two German drug salesmen who sat at our table. They were watching three Chinese boys play at "sailing ships" in a puddle of water in a corner of the Hostel yard. The "ships" were pieces of board, narrow and perhaps two feet long. For motive power the boys had caught rats and nailed their tails to the boards. Wary of being bitten, they placed the ships at the edge of the puddle and gave them a shove, as I have seen children do with sailboats in Central Park. One German complained of the Chinese cruelty to animals and, unable to control his wrath, rose with an oath and started after the boys. But they grabbed their boats, the rats dangling, and escaped.

The German was a big fellow with a cropped head, a typical Nazi, stern and brutal. Everyone laughed at him, even his German companion, who said, "Heinrich, we sit here and wait for the Japs to blow us to hell, and you swear at kids who torture animals."

"Yes," he replied in German, "there is death too in Europe, but that is war. I cannot bear to see animals tortured."

The sentimental thug, I thought, and recalled O. Henry's story of the detective who, by kicking a dog, provoked a murderer into self-betrayal. O. Henry's moral was, seemingly, that those who are sentimental about animals are capable of any cruelty to their fellow men.

With the terrifying scream of the emergency alarm, the lights died, leaving only a few oil lamps in huts nearby. These, too, quickly vanished. The crowd melted, leaving only Wu, Maria, and me. I told Wu to remain where he was and to watch the entrance. If the planes came suddenly, he was to warn us.

"Come on, Maria," I said and took her hand. It was cold and she was shivering.

Upstairs, I unlocked the refugee's door without knocking, opened it, and ran my flashlight over the room. "Work fast," I whispered. "I'll stand guard outside." I closed the door upon her.

In America it would be sufficiently hazardous, even with authority, to open a man's baggage, but in China it might be vastly serious, especially as I was under suspicion. If the search proved unsuccessful, the only witness to the honesty of my motives would be Wu, who would carry little weight with the Donkey.

Maria remained inside an uncomfortably long time, and I

had opportunity to curse the day I had ever come to China to take a thankless job, one in which my honesty and loyalty were so repeatedly questioned. Also, I could hear the sound of planes overhead, whether Chinese or Japanese I had no means of knowing.

What was Maria doing and why was she so long about it? Two minutes, I thought, should suffice to examine each piece of baggage. Eight minutes should be enough for all, and surely twenty minutes had passed. The bombers must be upon us at any moment.

The door opened, and I fairly jumped with relief. Maria was breathing audibly and fast. I locked the door hurriedly without turning on my flash and led her to the top of the stairs. I descended alone to a nervous Wu, who said the houseboy was nowhere about. Somewhat reassured, I returned to Maria and helped her down the stairs. She was weak and trembling.

Half a dozen brave souls were gathered at the dugout entrance, waiting for the sound of bombers. I found a chair for Maria, who dropped into it and bowed her head.

A deep-throated roar came from the north. *"Fei chi lai,"* cried the coolies and rushed frantically for the cave. I got Maria down the stairs, which were lighted by a candle, and then returned to Wu. We two alone remained outside. I, having been brought up in a mining district, could see that the timbers of the Hostel dugout would not withstand a hit. Wu, an engineer, shared my lack of confidence. With Maria we could do nothing. She wanted only to get underground.

"Find anything?" Wu asked as we stood there waiting for the bombs to fall.

"I don't know. I had no time to ask. But I think so, because Maria is scared to death."

"You don't look too cool yourself," Wu remarked with obvious truth.

I admitted to a slight sense of strain and mopped the sweat from my face and forearms.

The searchlights were all alive now, probing the heavens with their silver scalpels. Suddenly they found and held a squadron of planes flying much higher than usual. They were sweeping across the lower city, and we seemed safe enough. Guns roared at them, but they swept inflexibly on, thirty-six in echelon, to disappear in the south. Two more waves followed quickly.

"What do you make of it?" I asked. "Not a bomb was dropped."

"It is rumored that Wang Ching-wei has promised there will be no more bombing if the Chinese will make peace. If we do not, we are to be blown to hell. This is — what do you say? — a demonstration, a warning."

I thought sadly of Fidelity, wishing that I had known her better and that we had given and taken confidences. We had worked too secretly for our common cause, and thereby, I felt, she had come to her death.

A huge red light was run up on a pole near my office, indicating that the planes were still headed away from Chungking. If no more were on the way, the all-clear sirens would soon sound. I went into the dugout and found Maria, pale and drawn. I helped her up the stairs and into the car, which Wu had found. We sat there waiting for the all-clear, and Maria began to talk, but I pinched her arm to keep still, for I was not sure how much the chauffeur might understand. Nor at my apartment later would I let her talk until I made sure Lao Han was not at the door listening, as was his custom. Reassured, I turned to her. She was not the confident girl I had known, but she smiled wanly.

"He has a wireless," she said in a low voice.

"In which piece of baggage?" I demanded eagerly.

"In the heavy brown one — it's full of wireless stuff."

Both Wu and I shook her by the hand. I brought out a bottle of brandy. "*Prosit,*" she said, and, after a stiff shot, looked much better.

"I was so nervous," she confessed, "I shook so I could hardly open the baggage. And I thought I never could get the locks closed again."

I refilled her glass. *"Prosit!"*

She turned on the gramophone. Always after a few drinks she wanted to dance, and obediently I rolled up the cheap rug and pulled the table to one side. "You first, Wu," I said. He had studied four years in Germany, spoke fair German, and, like all Chinese educated abroad, danced well. The Chinese love white women — until they marry them.

Maria, I thought, deserved to be as happy as we could make her, and Wu and I alternately danced and poured drinks. We had reached an enjoyable pitch of hilarity when someone banged on the door. I cut off the gramophone and opened the door. There stood the Donkey. He looked as sour as a persimmon, and my hilarity instantaneously vanished.

"Hao pu hao," I said and bowed. Ignoring me, he brushed in and spoke to Wu peremptorily in Chinese. Wu, struck coldly sober, turned a sickly greenish yellow, like an unripe apple. He turned to Maria and said in German, "We have a conference. Please go into the back bedroom and close the door."

We were obviously in for something, but the more I thought of what we had done and of the Donkey's suspicions and high-handed actions, the angrier I became. I had my own ideas about handling the refugee. I'd let him send enough messages so that I could decipher them. I'd make no arrest until the last moment and then bag both him and his fellow spies.

"Keep your head, Adviser," Wu admonished me, "or you'll lose it and mine and Maria's, too. He has armed guards downstairs and has come to arrest you and Maria."

"Go on," I said. "What else?"

"He says the wireless at the German compound is giving out strong signals and is being answered. Messages in both directions have been intercepted. You and Maria are being held for investigation."

"Here?"

"No, in prison. I've told him nothing. Think fast. You know Chinese prisons. Anything can happen in them."

The Donkey, eyeing me impatiently, spoke again to Wu.

"He wants to know," Wu said, "if you have anything to say."

"No," I said, pouring myself a drink. "You go ahead and tell the whole story from beginning to end, how we planned to locate the sender, your part in lying out at night with the mosquitoes, and what Maria found under our direction. And after you finish the story, tell him that if he calls the guards, he will not leave this room alive." I took my revolver from my pocket and laid it on the table beside me. "You tell him that."

There ensued a long and animated discussion. While it was going on, I opened the bedroom door and looked in. Maria was on the bed, asleep. I pulled off her shoes and closed the door again. The Donkey, I thought, was weakening. I took up the gun and began to play with it. Then, as the Donkey eyed me uneasily, I shot off the neck of a bottle of brandy. He turned pale and said a few words to Wu.

"You and Maria are under house arrest," said Wu. "The Donkey will send men to the Hostel. When the refugee returns, he will be arrested, and if it is found that there is a wireless in the room, the house arrest will be lifted."

Wu looked hopefully at me. We had, he seemed to imply, escaped the worst. But the Donkey's stupidity and his interference in my plans left me coldly furious.

"You may tell him," I said, "that if the refugee is found guilty, the Adviser, in justice to his honor, will go to Number One or, in his absence, to the Generalissimo himself, to report the insults that have been heaped upon him."

Wu talked, and I could see that the Donkey was torn between disbelief and fear that what I threatened might come true.

"The general says," Wu translated, "that if he has been unjust, he will be the first to apologize."

"Damned nice of him," I replied. "Just to make sure he doesn't double-cross me, you're to go along with him."

Waiting for them to return, I fell asleep. Lao Han awakened me. "The general has come," he said in Chinese. There was this time no pounding on doors but a ceremonious announcement. I told Lao Han to show the general in. The Donkey, standing in the doorway, bowed respectfully, and Wu, behind him, grinned.

"The general offers his apologies," Wu translated. "The Honorable Adviser has displayed great skill and patriotism, and the miserable refugee is already in prison and his radio seized. He is awaiting trial."

It would be some trial, I thought, if the poor wretch was not indeed already dead. I asked Wu about this, and he said no. The refugee had been seized as he entered the Hostel, but before arrest he had swallowed a paper. The wireless was intact in the brown suitcase, as Maria had said.

"Let's go," I said and on the way to the prison picked up the Service doctor, whom I asked to bring, in lieu of a stomach pump, a Chinese drug that would make the man throw up. The refugee objected, but guards opened his mouth and held his nose as the doctor poured some vile concoction down his throat. He retched and retched until at last he threw up the paper. I examined it eagerly but the stomach acids had eaten away the writing, and I had no equipment with which to restore it.

They had placed the poor devil in a cage with all the scum of Chungking, who looked on curiously while he retched. Convulsed with stomach spasms, he held to the steel bars of the cage. Finally he became quieter and sat on the stone floor, his head in his hands.

"Tell the Donkey," I said to Wu, "that I want to talk to the prisoner alone." And the Donkey, eager now to placate me, consented.

I had the prisoner placed on a bamboo cot and there let him rest. After a time he opened sickly eyes to me.

"We are both white men in the Orient," I said. "Because

you're a white man, I'll try to save your life if you tell me everything."

"I have nothing to tell," he said in a shaky voice. "Nearly all foreigners in China have radios." He licked his lips, dry from much vomiting.

I called to the guard for a glass of tea. When the prisoner had drunk, I told him to rest and lighted a cigarette for him.

"Foreigners have receiving sets," I told him, "but not sending sets. I put a direction finder on you, and you were sending. That means death."

"It isn't true," he said weakly.

"You know it's true. But true or not, you'll lose your head if you don't come clean. You're a Honduran citizen. You do not have extrality."

"But — "

"Just one more thing. I will learn the truth however much you may deny it. I'm going to place you under a drug that will force you to talk. I'll learn all about you, or much of it. You don't believe this, but nevertheless it's true. If you first confess, I can save your life. I'll give you the drug in any case. If under its influence you tell me what you tell me now, I'll say you have confessed everything and should not be executed." As he continued to hesitate, I added, "If you say nothing now, you're a dead duck anyway, even if the drug doesn't work. Guilty or innocent, you're already convicted. But because you're a white man and I'm a white man, I'll try to save your life."

I had little sympathy for the refugee (especially because he had himself suffered persecution and violence and should therefore feel for the Chinese, who were oppressed, as he had been). In trying to save him, I was thinking of other foreigners. The execution of a foreigner for spying would be known to every Chinese, high and low, and Chinese suspicion of foreigners, already great, would make life in China even more hazardous than it was. The government would understand how one white man could be bought to spy on them, but the Chinese as a whole would put us all in the same boat. Uprisings against the foreign devils had been known before.

"I have nothing to lose, I see," the refugee said, his lips white. Then he went on to tell me that he represented Shanghai tin interests and had been approached by the Japanese in Hong Kong. He gave me names and addresses of agents already known to us. He had been paid to photograph whatever he could, had examined the tin mine, and returned to Hong Kong. There, he had been given a large sum to come to Chungking.

When apprehended, he had bundles of Chinese, English, Hong Kong, and American money on his person — a total amounting to about $30,000 gold. His mission, he said, was to set up a wireless. When contact was established, he would then be told what further to do. He had swallowed the cipher and could not remember the day-to-day keys, depending on the paper for them. The cipher gave a schedule, different each day both for kilocycles and time of sending, so that he had felt reasonably safe from detection, knowing the lack of detection equipment in China. After he had made contact and had perfected his radio, he planned to move here and there to avoid attention. He had built up a fair sending and receiving set from parts he had picked up.

I said, "After your radio was set up and you had contact in Hong Kong, what were you to do?"

"I don't know."

"You expect me to believe that? They gave you thirty thousand dollars gold. For what?"

"I really don't know."

"You're foolish to say that. Your life is at stake. You must have an idea."

"I was to set up a station and make contact. Then agents would come to Chungking. The password would be arranged in cipher by wireless."

"What was the plot?"

"I don't know."

"You want your head chopped off?"

I gave him another cigarette, and his hand trembled as he lighted it.

"I had a feeling the Generalissimo was to be murdered or kidnapped."

"Why do you say you 'had a feeling'?"

"A word dropped now and then. They spoke to me in English or German, but when they spoke in Japanese, which I understand a little, the Generalissimo's name was often mentioned."

"What else?"

"I think they were going to use parachute troops to kill or kidnap him. I saw maps. From Ichang it's only two hundred and fifty miles. They kept pointing at Ichang and Chungking on the maps." He leaned back on his wooden cot, exhausted, his face drawn and white.

"Is that all?"

He nodded weakly.

"I'm going to have you drugged," I said. "If what you say then tallies with what you've confessed, I'll save your head, but you'll probably go to prison. You've still nothing to say?"

"No," he said, and I somehow felt he didn't care much what we did to him. Death is, after all, a quick out. Life in a Chinese prison could be much worse. I wondered if I did well to save his life. Usually I guess wrong, and I fear it was so in his case.

Under sodium amytal he repeated his story as he had told it before, and he was placed in a private cell and permitted to sleep.

It was close to daylight when the Donkey and I got back to my apartment; I ordered breakfast and looked in on Maria, who was still asleep. I said to Wu, "Ask the general what he's going to do with the prisoner."

"He says he's to be executed at sunrise."

"Say that again!" I said.

"Executed at sunrise."

The mania for executing spies, even in the Western world, is a mystery to me. A live spy in prison may be valuable. Dead, he is of no use to anyone.

"Tell the Donkey," I said, "I don't want him executed. I thought that was understood."

"He says," Wu translated, "that was not his understanding."

"Ask him if he wishes me to tell Number One that while in the course of duty in running down a spy I was placed under arrest."

"He says he has apologized. Is that not enough?"

"No. The Donkey has been very stupid. The spy should not have been arrested. He should have been watched. Then we might have apprehended his confederates when they came to Chungking. I shall tell Number One that, as well as that I have been insulted."

Wu and the Donkey talked this over while I ate my scrambled eggs and coffee.

"The general says," Wu reported at last, "the prisoner is yours."

"Then tell him to get the hell out of here and cancel the orders of execution."

At the Hostel that morning there was great consternation among the foreigners. From them I got a picture of the refugee's arrest, of the Chinese gendarmes coming in and lining up the foreigners. There were rumors that the refugee had a radio, that he had been executed, that all foreigners might at any moment be placed under arrest. This I overheard with one ear while I could see them looking askance at me, surmising what I might do, hoping I might say something. Some, I knew, hated me. Others feared me. I pretended complete ignorance of the whole affair. I might have been more popular in Chungking had they known the part I had played. My mind was too filled with thoughts of the refugee to care much for their opinion of me. Had I condemned him to a life of misery? It was almost gladly I remembered that prisoners were not taken to dugouts during raids. The Japanese bombers might effect the release I had denied him.

· Chungking, May 1940

THE SITUATION IN EUROPE has given all of us the jitters. Hitler's armies are invading the Lowlands, and Holland has folded up. Life here in Chungking, while white men die in Europe, has become intolerable. I went to the French embassy and volunteered for service in France. The embassy cabled at once to Paris, and I am impatiently waiting an answer. China cannot hold me, for when my contract expired last March, I refused to sign another and am working on a day-to-day basis. The great Captain Georges Painvin must be back at his old job in Paris, doing his old tricks. I think he would like to have me with him. The little I know about ciphers I owe to study in France under him during the World War. It would be good to work again with skilled cryptographers, with up-to-date equipment, and with men of decision. I'm pretty well fed up here.

At noon every day a crowd gathers around the Hostel radio for the news broadcast from Saigon. The play of emotions on different faces — American, French, Dutch, British, Belgian, German, Polish, Russian — is interesting to watch. Though we are few in number, many nations are represented, and despite their conflicting reactions to the news, they contrive to remain outwardly friendly. But when the Queen of Holland deserted her people and fled to England, there was no silencing an American munitions salesman.

"What a cowardly bitch!" he cried.

"Oh," I said, "when it gets tough, all the leaders run — Napoleon, William II, Beneš — "

"Sure," he interrupted, "the men run, but I expected more of a queen."

I couldn't at the moment think of any other woman leader who had deserted her people to what will be slavery if Hitler meant what he said in *Mein Kampf.* And no one else disputed him, not even the Dutch minister, who probably thought less harshly of his sovereign. He turned the conversation by asking to see my fountain pen, which the Service had given me on my birthday. He admired its streamlined grace, and I told him, as I had been carefully informed, that it cost $40 gold or about $1200 Chinese. I place small value on things I carry in my clothes, for I invariably lose them, but I didn't say so when he offered to buy it. I said I couldn't sell it or I'd lose face, but that I might trade it for some of his good gin. He offered me four bottles, and being sick of the Chungking product and not wishing to appear grasping, I accepted. I told Wu and Ling I had lost the pen, but I think they smell a rat.

At the time the radio announced the flight of the queen, it reported that President Roosevelt had been granted another $100 million gold for defense. The comment at the Hostel was that they wished he'd stop selling gas and steel to the Japanese, for the feeling among us is that we'll soon have American steel about our ears, although the bombers have dropped nothing recently. It's all very mysterious. The American newsmen look wisely at me, as if I knew the answer, and hazard the guess that Wang Ching-wei has made peace proposals and that the parade of bombing squadrons is a threat of what will follow if the Generalissimo doesn't yield. Wang is merely wasting time and gasoline if he thinks the Generalissimo will ever give up. He'll retreat to Tibet rather than that. The newsmen could spend their time more profitably by getting about in China and sending home news stories rather than canned releases and futile speculations.

It has been raining for three days. Every time it rains, a few hundred coolies die when huts along the face of the cliffs collapse. The coolies are too shiftless even to build a secure place in which to live. I am not surprised. It's nothing for a Chinese chair or bed to collapse under you. When I tried to get a new spring put in my watch, the stupid watchmaker took a hammer and chisel to open the back, which anyone could see was screwed on. They weld a broken car spring and it breaks again at the first bump. For a boat paddle, they wire a piece of board to a stick. A knife or a fork breaks at the handle if you bear down on it — and some of this meat is pretty tough. These surely are not the breed that fashioned the famous Chinese porcelains. The Generalissimo will be a miracle man if he wins the war with such helpers.

All of my mail comes from Hong Kong, where, of late, it has been censored. It makes me mad as hell that England takes advantage of her far-flung empire and, because of a war in Europe, censors the mail of a neutral on the opposite side of the globe. I wrote the Hong Kong censor the following letter, not with much hope of doing any good but largely to blow off steam. However, if they will but take me off the suspect list, it will aid me in flying to Paris if my services should be accepted.

Hong Kong Censor,
Hong Kong.

Dear Sir, Madame, or Miss:

Looks like you've got me on that famous English suspect list. Don't blame you much. But there's no mystery why some of my mail is addressed to Herbert Osborn and some Herbert O. Yardley. The latter is correct. The double name is a Chinese idea — they don't want the Japs to know I am here in Chungking. The Japs already know it, but that makes no difference to the Chinese. A Hong Kong censor, even though British, should understand that. Really it's not my idea at all.

You'll find me in your *Who's Who*. I'm not a German-American. My forefathers came from England in 1725 and fought in the

Revolutionary War (a dubious recommendation, perhaps) and in the Civil War. In the World War, I was in charge of Military Intelligence Number Eight, handled censorship, secret ink, ciphers, and all that sort of thing. I was a military observer abroad and knew very well your Collins in your secret-ink labs in London, also your Major Hay in the War Office, etc., etc., etc.

Please consider a moment: What could a person in America writing to me in China, or vice versa, say in a letter that would be of value to Germany, with whom you are at war? Or do you just love to read personal mail?

My real identity is known to your embassy and consulate here. They know what I am doing. And so do you. So if you must open my letters, open them. But it would be nice of you if you'd take me off your suspect list . . .

All hell popping now for two days. I'm writing by vegetable-oil lamp — scarcely a lamp but a kind of saucer full of vegetable oil and a cotton wick. The electric lines are down and I can buy no candles.

Monday around noon we were all at the Hostel during an alarm. Thirty-six bombers approaching from the northwest headed toward the city, the Hostel in their line of flight. Everyone dived into the dugout in the corner of the grounds, except another chap and me. I stood at the entrance, watching them, and drew a breath of relief when they passed overhead without dropping a bomb. Wang Ching-wei, I thought, is keeping his promise. Then came the terrifying scream of bombs, and I plunged flat into the red mud, heedless of my white clothes. Hundreds of explosions, or so I thought, rocked the earth, and debris showered about me. I thought it would never end, and I must have been holding my breath, because when the explosions ceased, I gasped for air.

Thirty yards away, the Hostel was in ruins. The air was thick with powdered brick and plaster and the smoke from burning huts, automobiles, and trucks. I yelled to those in the dugout that the planes had passed, forgetting that the second and third waves were yet to come and that the sky was too full of smoke to see their approach. Only when, a little later, I heard explosions downtown did my apprehension disappear and I felt safe again.

The roads were so blocked that it was impossible to drive. I walked to my office, to find my fine chateau in ruins, smashed by direct hits, and the arch that read "Sweet Waters," my favorite hiding place, wholly demolished. A few coolies had been killed, but all my students were safe, though pale and trembling. No papers were destroyed, for the students always sat with a suitcase or box beside them, and at the first alarm the important documents were taken to the Monks' Cave. In the town many people were killed, but mass killings have become a commonplace in this war.

Some of the huge stones of which the chateau was built had been blown, intact, as much as two hundred yards away. The Buddhist temple, where the refugee children stay, was miraculously untouched, except for the outbuilding used to house medical supplies. The Russian, French, and English embassies, lying in the direct path of the bombers, all had been badly hit. Doubtless, ambassadors in Tokyo will make representations and the Japanese will express polite regrets with much bowing and show of gold inlays. Diplomacy must be an amusing occupation.

The Service has moved my office and the sleeping quarters for students to a building close to my old hut. They are frightened and cowed and look to me for leadership, which I cannot give. All I can advise them to do is to stay underground, for I'm convinced that we are in for bombings unprecedented in history.

The foreigners made homeless by the destruction of the Hostel have moved across the river to the Chungking Club, where I was blackballed, and sleep on the floor. Only a few have mosquito nets, and the mosquitoes over there are terrible. The APC, Asiatic Petroleum Corporation, which owns or leases a large compound, also took in several. Ling, Wu, Maria, and one of my translators live with me, or I would have taken some in, too. There are several foreign missions here that bought or leased compounds in Chungking several years ago. A few still stand, despite bombs and fire. One, which could sleep twenty people, was closed by the mission director, who has removed his precious hide to another compound beyond the First Range, where he will be completely safe. Close to the APC is an American oil compound capable of housing fifteen people. The manager has closed it and removed to a place of safety. I sent word to the Hatchet Man by Ling, suggesting that these places be opened by official demand. But he is afraid of criticism in the foreign press if he does so. If I were the American ambassador, I'd cable the church that controls the mission and the oil company that refuses to open its compound and by publicity shame them into doing the decent thing. But that is too much to expect, for the American embassy has yet to invite anyone even to sleep on the porch. Is it any wonder that the yellow man hates us?

· Chungking, June 1940

*F*RANCE HAS FALLEN TO HITLER, and though we in China live in a ghost world, drained of all emotion, it is hard to think of a Europe in which there is no France. Word of the surrender came as I was preparing to fly to Paris. The world is in chaos. The Japanese, growing bolder each day, heap insults and torture on English and Americans alike in Japanese-controlled China. All women are being evacuated from Hong Kong. War is certain. And I am undecided what to do — whether to remain here or return to the States.

In Chungking the situation worsens with each bombing. The bombers come in four waves, with long intervals between, so people must live underground for eight and ten hours at a time. Everyone is irritable and quarrelsome. Food is short. We drink Yangtze water and we are lighted at night by Chinese oil lamps. For the first time, my guards earn their pay, since each day they must pack my papers, clothes, radio, gramophone, and typewriter into a cave. On some days and even nights they make the trip several times.

There have been explosions and fires on all sides of my apartment, but it still stands, though the plaster has been knocked from walls and ceiling and all the window glass is gone. There are huge holes in the roof made by falling debris, but no one troubles to repair them.

I miss the two children, aged two and three, daughters of the family on the first floor. Their *amah* nurse taught them to speak to the foreigner. Whenever they saw me go or come, they would wave and call out, "Good-bye." They thought my name was Good-Bye. Both of them were killed, together with their nurse, by a falling building a short way up the narrow street.

Happily, I now have only myself to look out for. Maria, after a few tears, got away by plane for Hong Kong and Shanghai, which was what she wanted. However, it is sufficient to look after myself, for my feet are badly infected from mosquito bites. I have a running sore on each foot and fear blood poisoning. The Chinese doctors have all run away again, but last night Ling found some Epsom salts at a druggist's, and I have become my own physician. I soaked my feet most of the night, boiled some old rags for bandages, and bound them up. This morning I hobbled down the stone steps to the Yangtze — the chair coolies have fled also — and took a ferry to the gunboat, where the ship's doctor, Dr. Turnipseed, treated the sores and bandaged them with gauze.

The commander asked me to luncheon. The chow was very good — canned creamed beans, oyster dressing, and cherry pie with ice cream. Best of all was the ice water. Aboard ship, they generate their own power and make their own ice. The ice plant in Chungking has long since gone up in smoke. Schwer, however, still does well with Chungking gin and synthetic pop.

I stayed on the South Bank while four squadrons of thirty-six bombers each plastered the city, and I got some fine pictures of mushrooming bursts. When the clouds of dust and smoke and debris lifted, I was relieved to see my apartment still standing. I returned, to find the servants sweeping up the floor covered with the dust of explosions, now part of the daily routine.

2

Shon Ging, the pretty Chinese girl whom I met at the Hatchet Man's quarters when I first arrived in Chungking, has come back from Chengtu to visit her parents, who now live on the First Range. She dropped in to see me on her way across the river. It was Saturday afternoon. Wu had gone to the South

Springs, my translator was visiting his family downriver, and Ling, I could see, was anxious to get away somewhere, though I'm supposed to have an interpreter always at hand, in case the Donkey or the Hatchet Man wants me.

"I'll be back Sunday afternoon," Ling said at last.

"You're leaving me alone?"

Ling looked reflectively at Shon Ging, unruffled despite the heat and seemingly much more grown-up than when I had seen her last.

"I want to visit my family," Ling said. Then rapidly, so that Shon Ging could not understand, and with a sly look in his eye: "Chinese man likes woman on Saturday night."

I told him to run along, then went to my bedroom, sponged off, bandaged my feet, and changed my clothes. I sat beside Shon Ging, who looked at my bald head and frowned.

"Are you sick, Herbert?" she asked.

"Sick? No, but my feet hurt."

"I don't mean your feet," she said. "It's your head. It doesn't shine."

"I put some powder on it," I told her.

"Oh," she said, "I thought you might be sick. In China we say a man is sick if head does not shine."

I took my handkerchief, already moist, and wiped my bald head. "How's that?" I asked glancing at my shining head in the mirror.

"That is fine." She nodded.

It was stifling inside and I suggested that we take a ride out on the Chengtu Road to cool off.

"We'll get back in time for you to eat here and for you to cross the river and reach home before dark."

When she agreed, I told her to follow me at a distance until we reached the car so that there would be no vulgar insults from the coolies. Once in the car, she would be safe from them, and from the police, who now and then arrested Chinese girls alone with foreigners.

I should have known better. An air raid blocked us out on

the Chengtu Road, and it was well past midnight when we got back, hungry and eaten by mosquitoes. Lao Han served us dinner with yellow wine by the smoking Chinese lamps.

"It's too late to cross the river," she said. "I'll stay here until daylight."

Next morning when I awakened the sun was up. I looked in the bedroom, but Shon Ging had already gone.

Ling returned late Sunday night. I heard him talking outside with Lao Han, the wash *amah,* and the chauffeur. Ling entered with a grave face.

"Did Shon Ging stay here last night?" he asked.

"Yes," I said. "We were trapped on the Chengtu Road during an alarm and returned too late to get to the South Bank."

He shook his head.

"Shon Ging's father is high Chinese official. He is of old Chinese thought. Servants talk. When Shon Ging reached home, her father strangled her."

· Chungking, July 1940

I WAS SOAKING MY FEET in Epsom salts when Lao Han came in.

"A foreign gentleman has come," he said in Chinese.

It was an American military attaché with a roving commission in the Orient. I had met him once before. He knew who I was and what I was doing but had studiously refrained from asking questions. His message came like a thunderbolt.

"You're wanted in Washington at once," he said.

"What's up?" I asked, scarcely able to control my voice.

"War with Japan."

"I can't believe it," I said.

"It will break any time now. Japan has just demanded that all routes to China be closed — Indo-China, Burma. They may invade Hong Kong at any moment. The British are rushing evacuations. The Japanese have three divisions on the Kowloon border. I've talked with the embassy counselor. He says that, as an American working for Chinese Intelligence under an assumed name, you're subject to the death penalty if the Japanese capture you. You'll never make it through Indo-China or Burma. By flying over the Japanese lines to Hong Kong and taking the *China Clipper,* you may make it before it's too late."

"You're an optimistic devil," I said.

"Will you go?" he asked.

"Sure I'll go. I've been waiting for this."

"When?"

"Today. But I'll never get passage. Wealthy Chinese running away have the CNAC to Hong Kong booked up for months."

"I'll see that you get a ticket."

"For tonight?"

"Yes."

"How about my boss, General — — You know him?"

"Of course. I'll arrange your release."

Lao Han came in. "A foreign gentleman has come," he said. It was Dr. Turnipseed.

"It's okay, Doc," said the attaché.

The doctor opened a black case and began to take out a number of bottles and instruments.

"Now what?" I asked.

"Take off your shirt," Doc said. "You can't land in Manila or the States without typhoid, smallpox, and cholera inoculation certificates."

"But I already got them," I protested, "only thirty days ago," and got up to produce them.

"Chinese certificates," Doc said with a laugh, "are no good."

"They ought to be good," I said. "They made me sick as hell." And though I cursed him roundly, he gave me the works.

"I'd take them a dozen times myself," Doc said, "if it meant getting back home."

2

A busy day. A few minutes with the Generalissimo and the Hatchet Man and a farewell luncheon with many *kam-pei's*. Every servant who ever worked for me has showed up and kowtowed and has left smiling, after a generous *kom-sha*. A small quantity of foreign drugs, my riding boots, riding clothes, typewriter, tropical suits, and the like, I have divided among my interpreters and translators. I had a last *kam-pei* with my students, a last drink with Schwer, and a grudging *"mien tien shen"* with the Donkey. A word, too, with the Chinese gambler and his sing-song wife. A farewell chit and a few bottles of the

Hatchet Man's brandy went to Hugh of the embassy and the gunboat officers. On a last trip to the Bank of China I squared my loan with gold at thirty to one, their Shylock rates of 20 percent wiped out by the inflation.

In a few hours I take off for the States and a world rushing headlong to war.

MEMORIES OF
THE AMERICAN
BLACK CHAMBER

by Edna Ramsaier Yardley

> *Edna Ramsaier Yardley is the last surviving original member of the American Black Chamber, the secret codebreaking activity that for ten years, 1919 to 1929, read the diplomatic communications of many of the countries of the world. She returned to cryptology in 1941, in the Army's Signal Intelligence Service. She and Herbert Yardley were married in 1944.*

Edna Ramsaier at about the time she joined the
American Black Chamber

> Thousands of messages pass through our hands. The Black
> Chamber, bolted, hidden, guarded, sees all, hears all. Though the
> blinds are drawn and the windows heavily curtained, its far-
> seeking eyes penetrate the secret conference chambers at Wash-
> ington, Tokio, London, Paris, Geneva, Rome. Its sensitive ears
> catch the faintest whisperings in the foreign capitals of the world.

The reality was not quite as glamorous or melodramatic as it
was described in that famous passage from *The American Black
Chamber,* or at least it wasn't that exciting all the time. Cryptology is often a tedious, repetitious business, particularly when
you first begin trying to piece together the parts of a new code.
But that all changes when you are close to success, when you
know that in another few hours you will unravel the secrets of
a code that may have stubbornly defied solution for weeks or
months. That's how it was in the Black Chamber sixty years
ago, and perhaps it's still that way today.

If the work was sometimes routine, even dull, the people
never were. They were a brilliant, occasionally eccentric, group
of immense ability headed by the most colorful and fascinating
one of them all, the man I fell in love with and later married
— Herbert Yardley.

It began in the autumn of 1919, when the employment agency
sent me to 3 East 38 Street in New York to apply for a clerical
job. Instead of the office building I had expected, I found a
private residence, a four-story brownstone just off Fifth Ave-

nue. Unsure of what I might be getting into — I was only seventeen and this would be my first job — I rang the bell. The stocky, dark-haired woman who answered told me to return the next day. That was when I met Herbert, who, without telling me anything specific about the work, emphasized that it was very secret and that I was not to say anything about it, not even to my family.

My job, which paid about $20 a week, was to type code groups on 3-by-5 cards, about fifteen hundred cards a day. The code groups came from Japanese diplomatic messages, which Herbert was trying to solve; the cards I typed were studied for repetitions that might provide clues to decoding the messages. It took him five months to do it, but he finally solved the Japanese diplomatic code, and the first message was translated shortly afterward. Military Intelligence called it the "most remarkable accomplishment in the history of code and cipher work in the United States." To translate the messages that Herbert was by now producing regularly, we had Frederick Livesey and, later, Ruth Willson, who took over when Livesey accepted a job with the State Department. (Livesey, a gifted linguist, fluent in several languages, appears as "Charles Mundy" in *The American Black Chamber*.)

By that time I was helping to decode messages. I also kept files of everything the *New York Times* and *Christian Science Monitor* printed about Japan, especially Japanese foreign relations. Such information, particularly the texts of diplomatic notes, sometimes helped us guess the meanings of encoded Japanese diplomatic communications, our number one priority.

Once we learned the basic pattern, subsequent codes were not particularly hard to solve, even though the Japanese changed them frequently. Although we concentrated on Japan, we didn't neglect other countries, particularly Mexico and various South and Central American nations. We obtained copies of the messages from American cable companies through an arrangement Herbert worked out, possibly with the aid of the State and

War Departments, which paid our salaries and received the results of our work.

Our greatest success came during the Washington disarmament conference of 1921–1922, which was convened to determine the relative tonnages of capital ships of the major naval powers. By reading the secret messages between Tokyo and its representatives to the conference, we were able to keep the American delegation informed of Japan's strategy, particularly its willingness, if pressed, to accept a naval tonnage 40 percent smaller than that of the United States and Great Britain. The pressure on our small group was heavy — we often worked nights and weekends to keep up with the large volume of messages, which, when decoded and translated, were dispatched daily by courier to the State Department. But if it was exhausting work, it was also exhilarating; I'll never forget the feeling of elation as I rode home after a day of successfully decoding secret Japanese messages.

There were also some tangible rewards; for example, we all received Christmas bonuses in 1921 (mine came to $37), and Herbert received a letter of appreciation from Secretary of State Charles Evans Hughes. Shortly after the conference ended he left for Arizona to rest and recover from incipient tuberculosis. Early in 1923, he received the first of two Distinguished Service Medals, the Army's highest noncombat decoration.

I can add nothing to what has already been said about the reasons for the government's suddenly closing the Black Chamber in 1929. I do know, however, that to the six of us who were left it came as a bewildering shock. Herbert returned to Indiana to write and lecture; I returned to New Jersey; the others scattered elsewhere. The age of the American Black Chamber was over. But while it lasted, it was often exciting and always rewarding, and I am proud to have been a part of it.